Teaching *Julius Caesar*

Teaching *Julius Caesar*

A Differentiated Approach

Lyn Fairchild Hawks
Duke University

National Council of Teachers of English
1111 W. Kenyon Road, Urbana, Illinois 61801-1096

Staff Editor: Carol Roehm
Interior Design: Doug Burnett
Cover Design: Jody Boles
Cover Image: iStockphoto/Waltraud Ingerl

NCTE Stock Number: 51082

©2010 by Lyn Fairchild Hawks.

It is the policy of NCTE in its journals and other publications to provide a forum for the open discussion of ideas concerning the content and the teaching of English and the language arts. Publicity accorded to any particular point of view does not imply endorsement by the Executive Committee, the Board of Directors, or the membership at large, except in announcements of policy, where such endorsement is clearly specified.

Every effort has been made to provide URLs that were accurate when the text was written, but because of the rapidly changing nature of the Web, some sites and addresses may no longer be accessible.

Library of Congress Cataloging-in-Publication Data

Hawks, Lyn Fairchild, 1968–
    Teaching Julius Caesar : a differentiated approach / Lyn Fairchild Hawks.
        p. cm.
    Includes bibliographical references.
    ISBN 978-0-8141-5108-2 (pbk.)
    1. Shakespeare, William, 1564–1616. Julius Caesar—Study and teaching. I. Title.
    PR2808.H38 2010
    822.3'3—dc22

                                                                2009051787

Contents

Acknowledgments

I am grateful to teachers "in the trenches," working hard every day to differentiate instruction for our students. You are all artists making the best of challenging conditions to bring Shakespeare to life.

I thank Carol Tomlinson, Grant Wiggins, and Jay McTighe for their inspiration in the field and how they have shaped my teaching. I will always be grateful to Donna Dunckel, who inspired me to become a teacher, and to Angela Connor, who first inspired me with Shakespeare and truly challenged me to think in English class.

Special thanks to Bonny Graham and Carol Roehm, who shepherded this book into being, along with Kurt Austin, who believed in a second book.

Throughout everything, my parents Stephen and Katherine Fairchild have been my biggest cheerleaders; I thank them for keeping Shakespeare on the shelf and taking me to Stratford-upon-Avon. My sister Antonia Fairchild inspires me with her gift of creating a Forest of Arden wherever she alights. A special thanks goes out to my friend Teresa, who designed a beautiful website so teachers could receive many materials beyond this book.

And to my husband Greg Hawks, who gives me his constant love and support, thank you for all the trust and space to create!

Lyn Fairchild Hawks

Introduction

Making This Guide Work for You

Julius Caesar leads the Shakespeare canon because it captures timeless concepts: vaulting ambition, loyal friendship, deceptive charade, and political manipulation. Students can find parallels to current events, historical events, and personal dramas. Brutus and Cassius may sit in a desk nearby; Marc Antony and Caesar may rule the school or their city.

Just like the students who enter your classroom, you come to this book with your own readiness level, interests, and learning style. You have a certain level of experience with differentiation, a particular interest in certain aspects of *Julius Caesar* and Shakespeare, and a personal and distinctive teaching style with particular strengths. These lessons have been designed so that you can make these materials as individual as your teaching while keeping students and standards in mind. Make this unit your own with some of the following tips:

1. *Tier Your Learning.* If you are a beginning teacher or new to differentiation, consult the glossary (page xi) and additional readings (see Appendix A, page 209). Pay close attention to Notes on Differentiation at the end of each lesson. If you have intermediate or advanced experience, skim the glossary to learn this guide's acronyms, and then start reviewing lessons with an eye to how you might adapt them.

2. *Design Your Own Lessons.* This guide offers lessons for teaching reading, writing, speaking, performance, and research. Use these models as launching pads to create lessons suitable to you and your students.

Some Basic Information about Differentiation

Why Differentiate?

- All students should have access to Shakespeare.
- Higher achievement is possible for all.
- Shakespeare's plays should not be "covered." Students should interpret, adapt, and own these works.
- A variety of pedagogical approaches increases retention and understanding, resulting in higher student performance on both standardized and open-ended assessments.

- Rituals and routines allow the teacher to establish expectations, to check for understanding, and to build community.

- Diverse activities allow for student engagement, excitement, and choice.

- Tiered assignments address students' varying readiness levels and allow individualized progress toward core competencies.

- Investigating the play through a range of group experiences—tiered, whole-class, and mixed-readiness—allows students to construct new understandings while harnessing multiple intelligences, building community, and honing interpersonal skills.

- Adapting curriculum to the needs of the immediate group rather than following a standard approach each year makes Shakespeare meaningful for students.

Thinking Long Term about Differentiation

The challenge in differentiating instruction lies not only in the skills required to manage a busy classroom or inspire reluctant students; the challenge lies also in choosing appropriate strategies from a large buffet of pedagogical options. In addition, differentiation challenges your instructional abilities in areas beyond your comfort zone.

Here are tips to help you select strategies:

- Pick a few strategies or lessons to try this year, rather than trying to implement several. Evaluate the experience, and then modify activities for use next year. Each year add something new to your lesson bank.

- Pick strategies that spark your interest. If you adore the performance aspects, be sure to include multiple acting opportunities. If you are excited about iambic pentameter, focus on rhythm and rhyme during class discussion and readings.

- Stretch yourself in two ways: be a "Renaissance teacher," and embrace the big ideas.

  - You know the concept of the "Renaissance man," the multi-talented, well-rounded person. Likewise, educators must be curious about all their students' learning styles and interests and help students improve in a range of skill sets. If your teaching heavily emphasizes discussion and writing, where can you expand your repertoire? In performance? Cinematic analysis? Reading instruction?

  - No matter what skill set you teach, you will make it relevant by connecting it to a big idea. This phrase appears throughout this guide as a descriptor of the relevant and broad concepts that lead students to find themes and develop thesis statements. All students understand concepts such as love, envy, loyalty, and ambition; they live them. These concepts open the door for them to understand Antony, Cassius, Brutus, and Caesar. No matter whether you run a performance activity or a reading analysis, a writing mini-lesson or a Socratic discussion, keep in mind the "why"—the big ideas that drive the activity. This focus ratchets up an activity to a higher level of meaning, connection, and critical thinking.

- Challenge yourself, but don't overwhelm yourself. Stay within your zone of proximal development—your "learning curve zone"—where, like your students, you feel excited and motivated to learn more, sometimes frustrated, and always as if you are stretching, just not to the breaking point.

- Be a teacher-researcher. Differentiated instruction encourages observation and reflection, so keep notes of your impressions and insights and gather data on student progress and reactions. Record ideas for next year. Pursue reflective practice and scholar's seat opportunities at the companion website (http://www.lynhawks.com). Talk shop with colleagues and administrators.

Glossary for Differentiated Instruction

Differentiated instruction harnesses the best practices of educational research.

- It requires strategies in response to different readiness levels, interests, and learning styles.

- It addresses national and state standards to focus and elevate expectations.

- It designs lessons using themes and Socratic questions to prompt meaningful discussion relevant to students' lives.

- It offers engaging group activities, projects, and simulations that require critical thinking and that nurture a learning community.

The following terms will be used frequently throughout lessons, some using these acronyms.

Advanced student (ADV): A gifted student who performs above grade level and whose knowledge, skills, and/or pace of learning are more sophisticated than peers.

All students (AS): A designation for a learning goal applicable to all students (as distinguished from ELL, NOV, OT, and ADV).

Anchoring activities: Ongoing independent activities students may pursue throughout a unit; the go-to assignment when a student finishes a task early.

Big idea: A timeless concept appearing in many literary works, leading to themes and thesis statements.

Bloom's Taxonomy: Levels of critical thinking: remember, comprehend, apply, analyze, synthesize/create, and evaluate.

In 2001, Anderson and Krathwohl published a revised model of Bloom's Taxonomy using active verbs and outcome-based language. This guide's definition of Bloom's Taxonomy uses principles from both models. Notably, "evaluate" remains one of the highest levels of critical thinking, due to the requirements of criterion-based judgment, but analysis and synthesis (or "creation") are also high-level stages of critical thought. Ensure that all students encounter at least one of these three highest levels in assignments, activities, and assessments.

Close reader (CR): Reading guides that direct student comprehension and interpretation of text.

Compacting: Assignments and schedules for *ADV* students who demonstrate prior knowledge of grade-level content and skill and the ability to learn more quickly, deeply, and/or independently.

English language learner (ELL): A student who is a nonnative speaker and who performs below grade-level expectations.

Essential question (EQ): A thematic, investigative question that directs assignments and assessments (see Wiggins and McTighe's *Understanding by Design*).

Essential understanding (EU): A fundamental principle, theme, or generalization derived from the content and skills of the discipline; often an answer to an essential question (see Wiggins and McTighe's *Understanding by Design*).

Extension activity: An enrichment activity exploring concepts, knowledge, and skill at deeper levels while allowing students to explore interests.

Interest area: Student interests, such as talents, hobbies, expertise, and career goals.

Key word: An important word with strong connotations and connections to big ideas.

Learning style: The mode through which a student best absorbs, engages with, and constructs knowledge and skill, such as aural, kinesthetic, interpersonal, intrapersonal, verbal, and visual.

Mixed readiness (MR): A descriptor for activities or assignments in which students of varying interests, learning styles, and readiness levels complete a complex task.

Novice student (NOV): A student who performs below grade-level expectations and demonstrates a need for content and skills remediation.

On-target student (OT): A student who performs at or close to grade-level expectations for mastering content and skills.

Pretests and post-tests: Standardized assignments, activities, or assessments that measure grade-level knowledge and skill and that help diagnose whether students are ELL, NOV, OT, or ADV.

Readiness: A student's ability and preparedness to complete assignments (ELL, NOV, OT, and ADV).

Note the definitions of *big idea, key word,* and *theme.* Future lessons will teach students the definitions of concrete versus abstract diction and how to move between evidence and generalizations. These distinctions are key in the scaffolding of writing skills.

Skill strand activities: Interest area activities and projects asking students to demonstrate proficiencies, such as dramatic performance skills, Socratic discussion skills, creative writing skills, or cinematic analysis/visual-spatial skills.

Theme: Interpretations or arguments, as in essential understandings, generalizations, or thesis statements, derived from a big idea.

Tiered readiness (TR): A descriptor for activities or assignments in which students are clustered by readiness level to complete a task designed for a certain level of content and skill.

Tiered questions (TQ): Questions differentiated by readiness level and Bloom's Taxonomy.

Whole-class activity (WCA): A multisensory, multiple-intelligence activity designed to inspire, challenge, and motivate all students while emphasizing grade-level content and skills.

You can also find this glossary on the inside cover for convenient reference.

Getting to Know Your Students: Observations

Differentiated instruction encourages you to track students' growth through regular observations of their readiness, interests, and learning styles. Ask:

1. What are each student's strengths in reading and writing? (Consult standardized, classroom, and informal assessments. Recall direct observations.)

2. With what skills does each student struggle? Where are gaps requiring remediation?

3. At what grade level does each student perform?

4. How is each student both unique and typical when compared with his or her readiness group?

5. What are each student's interests and talents? (Consult The Bardometer at http://www.lynhawks.com, other interest inventories, and parent feedback. Use your observations and student interviews.) Which interests can you harness to expand learning opportunities?

6. What is each student's learning style strengths? (Consult learning style inventories and use parent feedback, your observations, and student interviews.) Which can you harness to expand learning opportunities?

7. What role does each student play during class? Leader? Follower? Entertainer? Witness? Mediator? (Use positive labels.) Assess social dynamics as you determine groups.

8. How has each student responded to Shakespeare or other complex texts in the past?

How often should you choose groups versus letting students choose? See if you can offer both options each week. When you divide students into TR groups, you should select, particularly in the beginning of a unit. You can then guide students with tips for making the best TR activity selections as the unit progresses, helping them to understand levels of activity challenge.

Companion Website

Visit the companion website to this book (http://www.lynhawks.com) for additional materials. While the lessons presented here are self-sufficient, you may wish to differentiate further using handouts available on the companion website.

- Reflective practice: Assess your experience and attitudes toward Shakespeare as well as your readiness level, learning style, and interests in teaching.

- The Bardometer, interest inventory: View an interest inventory to help you assess student interests that will aid their exploration of *Julius Caesar*.

To access the companion website, visit http://www.lynhawks.com, click on Shakespeare's image, and log in with your username (bard) and your password (caesar). Go to the Introduction section.

Assigning Reading: How Much? When? How?

Amount and Scheduling

In an ideal world, students would not only read every word of *Julius Caesar* but also comprehend and savor every line. Meanwhile, teachers feel pressure to translate all and explore all while rushing at top speed through the text to meet standards and pacing goals. How do you strike a balance? One solution is to ask students to savor key scenes. If students read and understand some words well, then less is truly more. Here are some tips as you make choices about reading.

This guide uses the Oxford School Shakespeare *Julius Caesar* because of its excellent text references, easy-to-read design, and strong prefatory and endnotes.

- Teach themes through scenes rather than plot through pages. A plot outline can be the first handout you give students so you can plan reading and class activities around key moments in the play that feed critical thinking: performance, discussion, essays, and projects.
- Require active reading by assigning short passages for study. Students will construct deeper meaning when they annotate, paraphrase, journal, and summarize. Select ten to thirty lines at a time, no matter what the readiness level, and assign thirty minutes of reading homework or classwork, which is enough time for NOV students to comprehend and annotate a short passage. CRs offer reading questions at different levels of Bloom's Taxonomy to aid comprehension and inspire appreciation. Reading supplements, class discussion, performance, and other activities can fill gaps in the plot.

The CRs appearing in this guide help students of all readiness levels appreciate key moments in the play while honing close reading skills. Note: ADV students don't need more verses to analyze but instead questions that demand deeper thinking.

Reading Supplements

When should you offer reading supplements? For all reading activities.

- ELL, NOV, and/or OT students can use *No Fear Shakespeare: Julius Caesar*. The editors run the traditional text on left-hand pages, and the right-hand pages provide a line-by-line modern translation. Another option is the e-book edition of Warren King's *No Sweat Shakespeare*, written in short-story style. Note: Supplements should translate but not interpret. The prefatory summary in *No Fear Shakespeare: Julius Caesar* offers character analysis. To avoid such giveaways, offer students only those sections that translate text.

- OT and ADV students can use a dictionary and a Shakespeare glossary. *Shakespeare's Words* defines words and allusions and conjugates Elizabethan verb forms.

Active Reading Strategies

Active reading leads to comprehension and analysis. What does active reading look like?

- *Marking the text:* As Mortimer Adler recommends in his essay "How to Mark a Book," encourage students to read actively by marking up the text. Copy key passages as homework hand-outs or post selections online so students can annotate using pencil and highlighters, give students different color sticky notes for marking school copies, or have them make personal electronic copies of online texts and use electronic highlighting. Use models of CR questions in this guide for ideas on how to direct student annotation.

- *Writing about the text:* Dialectical journals encourage students to dialogue with the text. Students copy key quotations in a left-hand column and then in the right-hand column ask questions, identify key plot points, analyze character and diction, predict consequences, connect to other scenes, and make personal connections.

Core Competencies

By the end of act 5, lessons will have explored the following English language arts skills. Each lesson labels knowledge and skill by tier (ELL, NOV, OT, and ADV). These tiers are suggestions, because how you define ELL through ADV depends on grade-level standards.

- What skills should ELL, NOV, OT, and ADV students master by the end of this unit?
- Considering when you introduce *Julius Caesar*, what can your students reasonably accomplish at this point in the year?

Review the following chart of core competencies on page xix. Which goals are essential in your school's and state's standards? Choose goals for each readiness level. Keep your goals simple and small (such as two per level) so you can measure progress at the end of the unit.

For example: *"I will help ELL students in: (a) learning how to translate and (b) learning how to find substantive evidence."* Ask no more of yourself or your students since you have four readiness levels to measure and teach. In addition, each skill requires many subskills, and you can plumb the depths of each skill area to make sure a student has truly mastered the objective before he or she moves on. One example is the reading skill of translation; see Handout 1.13, Tips for Tackling the Translation, on page 42, for the ten subskills required to master the process. Which subskills does each ELL student need most to master? There will be heterogeneity within each readiness level.

> Consider maintaining a skills checklist to mark as students show mastery.

The culture of standards, end-of-year tests, and curriculum guides might still pressure you to accomplish all in one unit, so have ready the core competencies your unit addresses and your lessons that will help each readiness level achieve mastery. It's hard to argue with such planning.

Unit Calendar

Consider devoting eight to ten weeks to this unit, for the following reasons:

1. The unit integrates core reading skills applicable to all literature study: annotation and analysis of key words.
2. The unit integrates core writing skills, such as developing topic sentences, building substantive evidence, and creating elaborative commentary.
3. The unit uses EQs and EUs to drive essays, discussions, and projects, which require quality time to investigate.

In other words, these content and skill objectives meet standards and are worth taking time to explore so your students can show mastery.

See the beginning of each chapter for a suggested calendar for each act.

Core Competencies

Reading	Diction	Characterization	Plot Analysis
—how to translate —how to annotate —how to write a dialectical journal —how to journal on a big idea	—how to find denotation and interpret connotation —how to find key words —how to balance concrete and abstract descriptions —how to use new vocabulary	—how to identify aspects of character —how to identify character motivations —how to interpret character traits	—how to identify types of conflict and obstacles in a plot —how to identify five stages of Aristotelian plot structure, according to Freytag's model —how to identify causes and effects
Persuasion & Literary Analysis	**Writing as a Process**	**Questioning**	**Figurative Language, Rhyme, and Iambic Pentameter**
—how to write a topic sentence —how to provide substantive evidence —how to present evidence using context and commentary —how to employ rhetorical devices —how to identify a theme —how to identify a motif	—how to structure a paragraph —how to prewrite —how to outline an essay —how to employ transitions —how to write a first draft —how to revise —how to edit —how to peer review	—how to distinguish types of questions —how to develop analytical questions —how to develop evaluative questions	—how to use simile, metaphor, hyperbole, paradox, personification, oxymoron, synecdoche, assonance, rhyme, pun, and alliteration —how to identify iambic pentameter and rhyme —how to use iambic pentameter to identify key words and emphasis

Act 1

Introduction

The Philosophy behind Act 1

During act 1 you can identify student readiness, interests, and learning styles; introduce core reading skills; and provide a fun, inspiring introduction to *Julius Caesar*.

- What grade-level objectives should your students meet? You will find that state and national standards overlap with these lessons' objectives. Use pretests to find out what students already know and can do.
- How will you teach translation skills and develop reading routines? Try this guide's prereading activities and TR assignments.
- How will you have fun? Sample the MR activities and WCAs.

As you craft daily lessons, keep these "ABC" principles in mind:

- A = Analyze (class is about critical thinking);
- B = Build community (class is about a community of learners); and
- C = Celebrate with theater (class is about performance).

What's in Store

In this chapter you will find activities to teach skills of translation, analysis, and performance, and activities to teach concepts in characterization, plot, and Roman history. You will also find:

- Assessments, including pretests and an act 1 quiz;
- Detailed lessons with several activity and homework options;
- Writing assignments and rubrics;
- Compacting projects;
- A historical mini-lesson; and
- Internet investigations.

At the end of this chapter, you can find tips for designing your own CRs with TR questions.

> Lessons 1 through 4 offer a measured introduction to the play and a practice of translation skills. If students are OT/ADV, condense or skip some mini-lessons.

Proceed slowly through act 1 of *Julius Caesar* so you can teach translation and active reading, helping students to build skills early to avoid frustration later. Before students open their plays, use pretests and prereading to prep students for independent work. You also need time to set up learning modifications, such as TR assignments and compacting.

Delete, expand, and combine lesson strategies as necessary; design sequences that work for you and your students. Sample lessons run between 50 and 140 minutes. Key handouts appear at the end of each lesson, while additional and optional handouts appear at the companion website, http://www.lynhawks.com. Notes on differentiation offer additional tips for lesson delivery.

Since diagnosis is ongoing, remember to observe students as part of your daily practice. An NOV student might achieve OT goals by the end of the unit; an OT student might achieve ADV goals. No one's assessment is static; everyone's zone of proximal development evolves.

After each lesson, reflect on your students' progress to adjust for the next phase.

- How did students perform in MR and WCA activities?
- Do TR activities suit student readiness? Should the challenge be increased or simplified?
- Which groupings were effective or ineffective? Why?
- Do activities meet student interests?

Keep in mind this principle of lesson design: what Carol Ann Tomlinson describes as "whole-part-whole" flow, a movement between groupings. Like a good story, each class should have variety, unity, and a beginning, middle, and an end. For example, a class might begin with a WCA, move to TR/MR activities, and then back to a WCA.

When differentiation seems like a tall order, take it lesson by lesson, day by day.

> To access the companion website, visit http://www.lynhawks.com, click on Shakespeare's image, and log in with username (bard) and password (caesar). Go to the act 1 section.

Companion Website

The scholar's seat is an optional "teacher warm-up" handout that can be found on the website. Respond to critics' interpretations of Caesar's character using strategies students will soon learn.

Suggested Calendar

This calendar is a sample guide for pacing lessons throughout the unit. Act 1 receives more time than others as you introduce students to skills and routines.

MONDAY	TUESDAY	WEDNESDAY	THURSDAY	FRIDAY
That Shows Character Homework: Character paragraph	*That Shows Character* Homework: Character paragraph & pre-play poll	*Taking a Stand* Homework: Handouts 1.7 or 1.8, or creative writing	*Tips for Tackling Translation* Homework: CR 1.15 A or B	*Tips for Tackling Translation* Homework: CR 1.15 A or B
Show What You Know: Pretest Homework: Journal or creative writing	*Sneak Preview* Homework: CR 1.22 A–D	*Sneak Preview* Homework: CR 1.22 A–D, and independent reading	*Hearkening Back to History* Homework: Speech preparation and independent reading	*Hearkening Back to History* Homework: Independent reading and persuasive paragraph pre-assessment
Building a Case Homework: TR independent reading	*Building a Case* Homework: TR independent reading	Perform excerpts of scene 2. Film clip. Homework: CR or independent reading	Perform excerpts of scene 3. Film clip. Homework: CR or independent reading	Act 1 quiz

Of course, these lessons are suggestions rather than prescriptions. See alternate approaches at the end of some lessons for different ways to approach the same subject.

Lesson 1: That Shows Character

Analysis (50 to 90 minutes)

Begin with a WCA, such as a mini-lesson or journal, and then move to
MR or TR partners so that students can conduct a CR analysis. End class
with a WCA discussion.

> This prereading lesson helps students learn skills of character analysis
> while meeting key characters in the play.

At the end of the WCA, students will know:

- there are six aspects of character: physicality; speech; thoughts;
  actions; family and origins; and other characters' speech,
  thoughts, and actions toward this character (AS)
- a protagonist is a principal character in literature (AS)
- direct characterization includes physicality, speech, thoughts,
  actions, and family origins. Indirect characterization is other
  characters' speech or actions (ADV)

Students will be able to:

- identify and analyze a character's traits using two of the six
  aspects of character (AS)
- distinguish direct from indirect characterization (ADV)

Students will understand:

- each quotation is rich with information about character (AS)
- literary characters can be complex (ADV)

Students will explore this question:

- What can we learn about characters from their speech and other
  characters' speech? (AS)

Materials and Handouts

Use the following handouts and materials during this lesson. Most appear at the end of the lesson (page 12) unless otherwise noted to be at
the companion website.

- Handout 1.1, Character Diagram; Handout 1.2, CR, That Shows
  Character; Handout 1.3, So You'd Like to Compact Shakespeare.
- The character diagram available as a visual, and a definition

of *character* posted: (a) *the mental, physical, ethical, and spiritual qualities (traits) of an individual*—"His character is complex"; (b) *personality, especially a funny one*—"What a character!"; and (c) *morality and integrity*—"He lacks character."

- Dictionaries and glossaries

Companion Website

Visit the act 1 section at http://www.lynhawks.com; click on Shakespeare's image and log in. Remember to log in with your username (bard) and your password (caesar).

- The Bardometer
- Handout 1.4A, Character Analysis Pretest Prompt
- Handout 1.4B, Character Analysis Pretest Rubric

Know a student with artistic talent? He or she can render a stock character figure for the character diagram (page 12) and make it a class handout.

Activities

STEP 1. WCA: Introduction, Mini-Lesson, and Journal (25 minutes)

1. Introduce the play as a suspenseful story with intriguing characters and
   a. meteors hurtling through the sky and lions pacing through a city,
   b. a psychic spouting omens,
   c. conspirators plotting to kill a leader,
   d. a hero—"the noblest man that ever lived"—murdered before witnesses,
   e. anxious wives pacing the floor at 3 a.m.,
   f. murderers bathing their arms in the victim's blood,
   g. a trusted friend turning on the friend he loves,
   h. people dying for the love of one another and country, and
   i. one man's ideals for a better country shattered.

In other words, tell students to get ready for some high drama.

2. Ask students who have not read or seen the play to make predictions about the play.

       a. TQ, AS: What part of the play I just listed sounds like it will be most interesting? Why?

       b. TQ, OT: Which events do you predict will be the crisis (climax)? Why?

       c. TQ, ADV: What act of a Shakespeare play is usually the climax? What themes do you already see connecting these plot events?

3. Explain that students will now: (a) get a sneak preview of key characters, and (b) analyze their own characters to practice characterization analysis. Ask a student to read the definitions of character on the board. Explain you will focus on definition (a). Review the six aspects of character as shown in Handout 1.1, Character Diagram (see page 12).

4. Ask students to imagine it is fifty years from now and they are being interviewed by someone authoring their biography. To prepare for this interview, they will analyze their own character using Handout 1.1, Character Diagram. Ask students to record significant details reflecting all six aspects of their character.

5. Ask students to share with a partner and then report about their partners to the class.

STEP 2. MR Activity: *Julius Caesar* Character Analysis, CR (30 minutes)

1. Explain that students will now analyze four protagonists in *Julius Caesar*: Cassius, Caesar, Antony, and Brutus. Define protagonist.

2. Explain the importance of solitary quotations and how one line can reveal an abundance of valuable information about the character speaking as well as other characters.

3. Ask students to work in MR partners to complete Handout 1.2, That Shows Character CR. Offer dictionaries and glossaries while they interpret quotations.

STEP 3. WCA: Discussion (20 minutes)

1. Ask MR partners to report character traits and defend them using the six aspects.

All students are eligible to answer TQs. Questions are labeled by readiness level to indicate whether they require prior knowledge or skill, but these labels are not prescriptive.

2. Ask TQs:

   a. (AS) What is a nobleman? A praetor?

   b. (AS) What aspects of character are revealed from quotations said by Julius Caesar? From quotations about Julius Caesar? Pinpoint words or phrases that illustrate each aspect of character.

   c. (OT) Describe Julius Caesar's traits using one or more adjectives. (Allow debate to find most appropriate adjectives. Repeat this process for another character.)

   d. (ADV) Which of the four characters seems most complex? How do you know?

   e. (ADV) What is the difference between direct and indirect characterization? Identify an instance of each. How do you know whose viewpoint to trust?

   f. (ADV) There are more than 550 lines in act 1. We've read fewer than fifteen. Why might these few lines matter when there are hundreds more?

Critic Harold Bloom credits Shakespeare with the invention of modern psychology, saying his understanding of what it means to be human makes his work unique for his time. How can you help students see the humanity in the characters?

Homework Options

1. To pretest for characterization skills, ask students to write a character analysis paragraph of at least 100 but no more than 250 words about Cassius, Caesar, Antony, or Brutus. Request that students include: (a) a clear topic sentence, (b) supporting details, and (c) elaboration on details. See Handout 1.4A, Character Analysis Pretest Prompt, at http://www.lynhawks.com.

Tips for pretesting: Explain to students that pretesting helps you tailor lessons to their needs. Assure students that if they demonstrate effort, they can earn straight credit for this assignment. Consider supervising this pretest in class.

---

2. If you haven't yet assessed student interests, use the Bardom-eter (http://www.lynhawks.com).

3. If you plan to use Lesson 2: Taking a Stand (page 17), ask students to complete Handout 1.5, Pre-Play Poll: Where Do You Stand? (page 23) and Handout 1.7, What's the Big Idea in *Julius Caesar*? An Interest Inventory.

4. ADV only: Review Handout 1.3, So You'd Like to Compact Shakespeare. Students who qualify for compacting should have already met key unit objectives or can more quickly and thoughtfully meet them. Give pretests from this guide and also look at achievement and aptitude tests (scores of 95th percentile and above). See your school's definition of *gifted*.

Notes on Differentiation

1. The day prior to this lesson, consider offering the "smart start option": a chance to preview the next day's readings the night before. Encourage ELL and NOV students especially to review Handout 1.2, That Shows Character (page 13).

2. During Step 1, you can model the character analysis process by sharing your own. Post these questions if students need help completing Handout 1.1, Character Diagram:

   a. What's an important thought you had today? (thoughts)

   b. What's a typical phrase or expression you often say? (speech)

   c. What is an important detail or trivia about your family, race, ethnicity, birthplace, religion, or anything else about your origins? (family origins)

   d. What is something someone said about you recently? (what other characters say)

   e. What is one of your distinguishing physical features? (physicality)

   f. What's a key action you took recently? (actions)

   g. How do all these details indicate your overall character? Name three qualities, or traits, you have. (topic sentence for character traits)

3. *Assessment of Character Analysis Pretests:* If you give this pretest, use Handout 1.4B, Character Analysis Pretest Rubric (http://www.lynhawks.com) to sort student work into four groups (ELL, NOV, OT, and ADV) or eight groups (ELL Tier 1, ELL Tier 2, NOV Tier 1, etc.). Sorting helps you plan for remediation and TR assignments. If you are comfortable with differentiation, try eight groups, as Tier 2 indicates students at upper ranges of their readiness level who may be able to move into a new

TR group during the unit. Students may also overlap across tiers: one who is Tier 1 in organization, voice, and style might be Tier 2 in character analysis. The rubric can help you decide which knowledge and skill each readiness level needs most.

4. Compacting students may pursue enriched and accelerated studies separately, with or without a mentor, and should return to class often for WCAs and MR activities, such as discussions, peer review, and presentations. You can mention the opportunity of compacting to all students, as described in Handout 1.3, So You'd Like to Compact Shakespeare (page 15), and then see who approaches you. Or you can hand it only to those you think qualify and who are likely to earn 80 percent or better on the preassessments. If you've never compacted curriculum before, limit your distribution to independent, resourceful, and quick learners with an A or B average. A profoundly gifted reader and writer whose learning will be slowed by daily lessons should be eligible for compacting Shakespeare. Add other criteria as necessary based on how you have taught prior units, such as an A earned on a certain essay or a certain level of reading proficiency. Criteria should be clear and fair, and keep in mind how such criteria will remain or change for future units. Have available Handout 1.12, Compacting Fun: Suggested Activities and Projects (page 31), so students can better understand project opportunities.

Help potential compacting students self-evaluate with these tips: "If you are highly motivated, compacting is for you. If you are passionate about the study of literature and writing, then compacting is for you." Broaden your criteria to students who are underachieving gifted if you have means to support them.

---

a. How often a compacting student participates in WCAs and MR activities is up to you. Compacting students can join WCAs, such as dramatic performance, Socratic discussion, and cinematic analysis. All students should build communication, teamwork, and leadership skills as well as hone visual-spatial and kinesthetic abilities in the opportunities afforded by WCAs.

b. Compacting students should pursue clear goals, receive ample time for projects, and get frequent feedback from you or another qualified mentor. Determine what "compacting out" means for each student who qualifies and develop a learning contract that reflects those objectives. Look above grade level, considering ninth-grade work for a seventh grader, or twelfth-grade work for a ninth grader. For all independent work, provide a learning contract for the student and parent to sign, the schedule with a task log for you to check, and rubrics for assessment. Schedule at least one conference per week if a student misses a significant amount of class. Seek the support of media specialists, parents, and other community mentors so that compacting students receive individualized attention.

ADV students are diverse in readiness levels, interests, and learning styles. A student should compact out of class activities when lessons review what a student has already mastered. Can a student comprehend Shakespeare's language more deeply than others? She may need to skip lessons analyzing plot and pursue an accelerated reading schedule and ADV CR assignments. Has a student demonstrated in-depth literary analysis but never read Shakespeare? He may be able to skip WCAs on essay writing and pursue an ADV essay topic. See Susan Winebrenner's book, *Teaching Gifted Kids in the Regular Classroom*, for more detailed guidelines and a sample learning contract.

---

   c. Projects for compacting students should be challenging acceleration opportunities (chances to practice higher level content and skills) or enrichment opportunities (chances to explore more deeply a subject or an interest).

   d. Provide opportunities for compacting students to present projects to the class.

Alternate Approach to Lesson 1

Lesson 1 relies heavily on verbal-linguistic abilities. To allow students to explore different learning styles while achieving similar objectives, consider alternate lesson options. Note these options rely on storytelling and design, two core elements of twenty-first-century thinking (Pink). When students creatively synthesize disparate elements prior to reading, they experience the roles of actors and playwrights designing plot.

Kinesthetic Activity: Divide students into MR groups and give each two quotations from Handout 1.2, Close Reader: That Shows Character. Directions: (a) Create a skit in which (1) one speaker of a quotation is the protagonist and (2) both quotations are spoken. (b) This skit should show an intense crisis scene that has some connection to Caesar's assassination. Make up any story that ties the two quotations together. (c) Choose three aspects (physicality, speech, actions, etc.) to represent your characters. (d) Involve all group members in performance. (e) Bonus given to skits that use Shakespearean vocabulary in all speaking. (f) Present skits. Audience members should analyze how well groups presented character aspects using quotations and performance techniques.

Visual-Spatial Activity: Divide students into MR groups and give each four quotations to translate and place in logical order to show how an assassination plot might unfold. A timeline, flow chart, or other visual representation can be used, along with symbolic illustrations for each quotation and a one- to three-word caption to represent a stage of plot. Groups present their charts to the class and explain the order, symbols, and captions. Audience members should analyze the logic of the plot design—how well quotations are linked in a cause-and-effect pattern.

Handout 1.1, Character Diagram

Teaching Julius Caesar: *A Differentiated Approach* © 2010 Lyn Fairchild Hawks.

Handout 1.2, Close Reader: That Shows Character

Directions:

1. Read the quotations and their translations.

2. Select a character to analyze. What can you learn about the character who is speaking? What can you learn about the character based on what other characters say?

3. Complete Handout 1.1, Character Diagram. Where information is lacking for an aspect of character, give your best guess based on what you already know.

4. Challenge: Identify which quotations are direct or indirect characterization—or both—and explain why this distinction matters.

- **CASSIUS**, a nobleman and senator: "Men at some time are masters of their fates:[1] The fault, dear Brutus, is not in our stars, but in ourselves, that we are underlings."[2] (act 1, scene 2) TRANSLATION: *We are responsible for our destiny. If we aren't successful, it's our fault.*

- **CAESAR**, a general: "Yond[3] Cassius has a lean and hungry look; He thinks too much: such men are dangerous." (act 1, scene 2) TRANSLATION: *Cassius looks lean and hungry. He thinks too much. Guys like him are dangerous.*

- **CAESAR**: "Cowards die many times before their deaths; The valiant[4] never taste of death but once." (act 2, scene 2) TRANSLATION: *Cowards humiliate themselves before they die, but brave people die only one time, like heroes.*

- **ANTONY**, a soldier and follower of Caesar: "Friends, Romans, countrymen, lend me your ears; I come to bury Caesar, not to praise him." (act 3, scene 2) TRANSLATION: *Listen to me, my friends, Romans, countrymen. I'm here to bury Caesar, not to praise him.*

- **BRUTUS**, a nobleman and praetor: "Not that I loved Caesar less, but that I loved Rome more." (act 3, scene 2). TRANSLATION: *It's not that I didn't love Caesar; I just loved my country, Rome, more.*

- **ANTONY**: "When that the poor have cried, Caesar hath wept: Ambition[5] should be made of sterner[6] stuff." (act 3, scene 2) TRANSLATION: *Caesar cared about the poor; perhaps we should wish this ambitious man were more cold-hearted.*

- **BRUTUS**: "As he (Caesar) was valiant,[7] I honor him; but, as he was ambitious, I slew him." (act 3, scene 2). TRANSLATION: *Caesar was brave and for that I honor him; but because he was ambitious, I killed him.*

- **ANTONY**: "When Caesar says, 'Do this,' it is perform'd." (act 1, scene 2) TRANSLATION: *When Caesar tells us to do something, we do it.*

continued on next page

- **CAESAR**: "Such men as he (Cassius) be never at heart's ease/Whiles they behold a greater than themselves,/And therefore are they very dangerous." (act 1, scene 2) TRANSLATION: *Men like Cassius are never content when they see someone greater than themselves, and therefore they are very dangerous.*

- **ANTONY**: "Fear him (Cassius) not, Caesar, he's not dangerous,/He is a noble Roman and well given." (act 1, scene 2). TRANSLATION: *Don't be afraid of Cassius, Caesar; he's not dangerous because he's noble and has a good reputation.*

- **BRUTUS**: "What you have said/I will consider; what you have to say/I will with patience hear." (act 1, scene 2) TRANSLATION: *I'll consider your words and listen patiently later.*

1. Fates: Destiny; gods who determine human life

2. Underlings: Person who is inferior or subordinate to another; level of slave or servant

3. Yond: Over there (indicating Cassius's location), as in "That Cassius over there . . . "

4. Valiant: The brave

5. Ambition: The desire for fame and power

6. Sterner: Harder, tougher

7. Valiant: Brave

Handout 1.3, So You'd Like to Compact Shakespeare

What Is Compacting?

Compacting is an opportunity to pursue advanced assignments in an independent learning schedule. Students who demonstrate they have already mastered objectives or can master them more quickly and deeply may be eligible. If a student "compacts out" of certain work, he or she will pursue enriched[1] and accelerated[2] studies instead.

What Makes a Student Eligible?

A student must meet three or more criteria to qualify for compacting.

1. Is able to read and understand an unabridged[3] version of the play.
2. Has performed and can easily translate several unabridged scenes.
3. Has seen the play live, watched more than one film version, and/or has read several original-language scenes from the play, and understands them.
4. Has already read and understood an unabridged version of another Shakespeare play.
5. Understands more than 80 percent of Shakespeare passages studied in class.
6. Can read the play independently without much coaching or reliance on translations.
7. Is eager to work at a greater level of challenge.
8. Possesses excellent literary analysis and writing skills.
9. Has a desire to design a unique course of study and personalized projects.
10. Has creative ideas and interests related to Shakespeare to explore.
11. Has earned a certain grade on prior tests or essays in this class.
12. Has earned a certain score on aptitude tests.
13. Works well independently.

If I Meet at Least Three Criteria: What's Next?

Earn excellent grades on plot quizzes for *Julius Caesar* and/or demonstrate proficiency[4] on a translation test. Meet any other required standards. Here are some tips:

1. If you've already read most or all of the play, review the play. You will then take the quizzes at one time. You must earn 85 percent or better. To prepare, spend time in the text and make outlines. Don't rely on study aids; translate on your own.
2. If you haven't read the play, read the first act of *Julius Caesar*. Don't rely on study aids; translate on your own.

continued on next page

Important Reminders:

1. Do not share your knowledge of these assessments with other students.
2. Compacting is not a permanent learning modification.
3. If you do not meet the expectations of your contract, we will revisit the arrangement.

Assuming I Pass the Assessments, What Happens Next?

When we conference, we will develop a schedule of assignments. You will work independently sometimes and return to class other times. Start a list of potential project ideas and questions you would like to explore.

Ideas for Compacting Projects

1. _____
2. _____
3. _____

1. Enriched: Advanced in terms of depth and interest level

2. Accelerated: Advanced, above grade-level expectations

3. Unabridged: Not shortened or changed for easier reading; the original version

4. Proficiency: Skill and expertise

Teaching Julius Caesar: *A Differentiated Approach* © 2010 Lyn Fairchild Hawks.

Lesson 2: Taking a Stand

Analysis (50 to 90 minutes)

Begin with a WCA mini-lesson, assign CR analysis, and end with WCA activity and discussion.

This prereading lesson helps students learn skills of diction analysis while previewing key concepts (big ideas) in the play.

At the end of the prereading lesson, students will know:

- the difference between concrete and abstract words (AS)
- that a big idea is an abstract noun and a timeless concept appearing in many literary works (AS)
- that theme is a conclusion about a big idea as represented in a literary work (OT, ADV)
- the definition of essential questions (OT/ADV)

Students will be able to:

- analyze a sentence to find the abstract concept behind it (AS)
- justify an abstract big idea using concrete examples (OT)
- pose essential questions (ADV)

Students will understand:

- big ideas relevant to daily life are at work in *Julius Caesar* (AS)
- complex themes emerge from essential questions (ADV)

Students will explore this question:

- Where do I personally stand on big ideas explored in this play? (AS)

Materials and Handouts

Use the following handouts and materials during this lesson. Most appear at the end of the lesson (page 23) unless otherwise noted to be at the companion website.

- Handout 1.3, So You'd Like to Compact Shakespeare; Handout 1.5, Pre-Play Poll: Where Do You Stand? Handout 1.7, What's the Big Idea in *Julius Caesar*? An Interest Inventory; Handout 1.8, Digging Up Themes in *Julius Caesar*; Handout 1.10, Act 1

Plot Quiz and other acts' quizzes as needed; and Handout 1.12, Compacting Fun: Suggested Activities and Projects.

■ Dictionaries and glossaries

■ Quotation posted: " . . . *How many ages hence / Shall this our lofty scene be acted over / In states unborn and accents yet unknown!*" (3, i, 111–113).

■ Number 16 from Handout 1.5 posted: "*An honest person is hard to find.*"

■ A taped line on the floor or the board with AGREE on one end, DISAGREE on the other, and UNDECIDED posted in the middle.

■ A definition of *concrete* (tangible, able to be experienced with the senses) and *abstract* (intangible, relating to ideas or concepts) posted.

Companion Website

See http://www.lynhawks.com for the following materials:

■ Handout 1.4B, Character Analysis Pretest Rubric

■ Handout 1.6, Recitation Regulars

■ Handout 1.9, Translation Test

■ Handout 1.11, Compacting Contracts and Schedules A and B

■ Big Ideas in the Real World: Barack Obama's Inaugural Address

Activities

STEP 1. WCA: Introduction and Mini-Lesson (15 minutes)

1. Collect character analysis pretest paragraphs if students completed them for homework.

2. Ask students to listen to you read the posted quotation from *Julius Caesar*. Then explain the context: men with blood-stained hands standing over a corpse of Caesar, and Cassius, one murderer, speaks. Ask for three students to read the quotation slowly, and ask each to choose a different word to stress (hence, lofty, unknown).

3. Ask students to translate this quotation using three strategies (see Lesson 3, Tips for Tackling Translation, in which these strategies are specifically taught; this is an informal pretest): (a) What is the complete thought (Where is the subject of the sentence? The predicate?); (b) What words do you already know?; and (c) What do words such as "lofty" and "hence" mean? Then ask for a restatement of the quotation in modern language. Possible translations: "This glorious scene will be replayed some day in countries and languages that don't yet exist!" or, the *No Fear Shakespeare* translation: "How many years from now will this heroic scene by reenacted in countries that

don't even exist yet and in languages not yet known!" (*No Fear Shakespeare* 111)

4. Introduce anchoring activities and the first option, recitation regulars. Distribute Handout 1.6, Recitation Regulars. Let students know they will need to apply these translation skills when preparing recitations.

Anchoring activities are ongoing independent activities, go-to assignments when a student finishes a task early. Offer several options; Handout 1.6, Recitation Regulars, available at http://www.lynhawks.com, is one that emphasizes public speaking. Later in the unit, you can pull names from a hat to have students perform daily.

---

5. ADV TQ: Ask students to connect this quotation to modern and ancient history (assassinations, conspiracies, ambitious leaders). Responses will show who possesses advanced interest in and knowledge of history.

6. Explain to students they will soon share pre-play poll answers with a partner and analyze the big idea behind statements—timeless concepts *Julius Caesar* explores.

    a. Ask a student to read aloud #16, "An honest person is hard to find."

    b. Ask students which word in the quotation indicates something tangible or *concrete* (what you can see, hear, taste, touch, or smell). Answer: "person."

    c. Which word is intangible or *abstract*, representing an idea, something you can't see, hear, taste, touch, or smell? Answer: "honest."

    d. Explain that a big idea is always stated as an abstract noun. Ask students to convert "honest" to an abstract noun ("honesty"). They have just identified a big idea. While reading *Julius Caesar*, they will explore questions raised by these concepts and convert them to themes—conclusions and generalizations of how this concept reveals itself in a literary work. Later they will learn how to move between evidence and generalizations, and *concrete* versus *abstract* will be key.

STEP 2. MR partners: CR analysis (10 minutes)

Ask students to complete Handout 1.5, Pre-Play Poll, independently (if not already done for homework). Ask them to share answers with a partner, explain choices, and identify big ideas behind as many statements as they can.

For a modern connection to big ideas, see Barack Obama's 2009 inaugural address in which he raised four big ideas that Julius Caesar explores, " . . . hard work and honesty, courage and fair play, tolerance and curiosity, loyalty and patriotism— these things are old. These things are true. They have been the quiet force of progress throughout our history."

STEP 3. WCA: The Human Graph and Reporting Big Ideas (30 minutes)

1. Ask volunteers to participate in The Human Graph, an activity in which five or more students take a stand on a taped line in response to pre-play poll statements.

   a. Read aloud a statement you want students to discuss. (Suggestion: Begin with #s 1, 4, and 8.) Ask five to seven volunteers to move to a spot—AGREE, DISAGREE, or UNDECIDED—in response to the statement.

   b. Ask one student from each position to defend it using concrete examples, such as current events or personal examples. Those at UNDECIDED can pose questions to others at different positions. Ask the class to help with examples or questions. Invite others to "take a stand." Be on the lookout for students who refuse to take a position until they can ask questions, and compliment this approach.

   c. Encourage definition and clarification of abstract words from the poll, such as *honest* or *stern*, using their own examples. Ask students who are seated to weigh in throughout the discussion.

   d. After discussion, ask if anyone wants to change positions.

   e. Consider discussing at least three statements.

2. Make a list together on the board of big ideas reflected in the pre-play poll statements.

3. Preview more big ideas in the play by listing them (use Handout 1.7, What's the Big Idea in *Julius Caesar*? An Interest Inventory. Review meanings of *ambition, caprice, constancy, idealism, fate,* and *free will*.

4. Ask TR questions.

   a. Which big ideas here and in the pre-play poll do you also see in the quotations from Handout 1.2, That Shows Character? (OT)

   b. Are there certain big ideas that seem to be more important than others? (OT)

c. Which big ideas are most relevant today in American society? Why? (AS)

d. Which big ideas connect? Link some to make a generalization or theme. (ADV) Examples:

    i. Patriotism is a form of loyalty.

    ii. Loyalty can come from courage or cowardice.

    iii. Envy can destroy the love and loyalty between friends.

This exercise previews skills needed for thematic literary analysis and thesis statements. Encourage students to convert nouns to adjectives or adverbs as needed. If a generalization seems shaky or unclear, ask students to explain reasoning with concrete examples. Encourage students to help one another build themes.

Homework Options

1. Assign TR homework: Handout 1.7, What's the Big Idea in *Julius Caesar*? An Interest Inventory (for ELL and NOV) and Handout 1.8, Digging Up Themes in *Julius Caesar* (for OT and ADV).

2. Ask students to choose and practice a passage for recitation (Handout 1.6, Recitation Regulars, available at http://www.lynhawks.com).

3. Other options:

    a. Assign the character analysis pretest.

    b. Ask compacting applicants to prepare for pretests.

    c. Give a creative writing assignment: Write a skit or story illustrating a big idea. Examples: write a scene in which one person is *envious* of a friend's *courage*. Write a scene in which one person is an *idealist* and the other a *realist* about *love*.

What should your quizzes assess? Included in this guide are sample assessments for acts 1 and 2 that include open- and closed-book portions. These test for basic plot knowledge, key reading and writing skills, and historical knowledge about Shakespeare and Caesar. Consider creating two versions, even though you ask compacting applicants to abide by the honor code, or using Tic-Tac-Toe (page 96) as an alternate assessment.

Notes on Differentiation

1. Remember the "smart start option" if you introduce the pre-play poll in class. ELL and NOV students may need extra time the night before to consider statements prior to discussion.

2. Compacting:

   - If you schedule qualifying ADV students for compacting, arrange a time to conference about expectations, to take quizzes (see Handout 1.10, Act 1 Quiz, page 29 and Handout 2.9, Act 2 Quiz, page 142 for models) and the Translation Test (Handout 1.9, Translation Test for Compacting, available at http://www.lynhawks.com), and to establish a contract and schedule. Adjust criteria and edit quizzes as needed to determine whether compacting students need to return to class for mini-lessons.

   - Help students preview compacting by sharing Handout 1.12, Compacting Fun: Suggested Activities and Projects, page 31. Where possible, help students develop project rubrics that reflect learning goals particular to each student. Use criteria from this guide's rubrics as a starting point.

   - Clarify when and how you are available to compacting students. Consider finding a mentor for ADV students who need special guidance or feedback. Media specialists, local professors, professionals in the field, or a college student or parent with a strong background in English Language Arts are potentially good mentors. For more ideas about arranging compacting, see Susan Winebrenner's *Teaching Gifted Students in the Regular Classroom*.

   - Some projects on Handout 1.12 are suitable for other readiness levels and might be excellent project options for OT students at the close of the unit.

Handout 1.5, Pre-Play Poll: Where Do You Stand?

Directions: This poll seeks your opinions. Decide whether you AGREE, DISAGREE, or are UNDECIDED about the following statements.

1. Sometimes you must assassinate[1] a leader to get a better government.
   AGREE   DISAGREE   UNDECIDED
2. The will[2] of the people is always best for a country.
   AGREE   DISAGREE   UNDECIDED
3. It's a good idea to heed[3] the warnings of psychics[4] or astrologers.[5]
   AGREE   DISAGREE   UNDECIDED
4. Power corrupts, no matter how ethical[6] a leader might be.
   AGREE   DISAGREE   UNDECIDED
5. You can love someone even if you kill them.
   AGREE   DISAGREE   UNDECIDED
6. A proverb: "The road to hell is paved with good intentions."
   AGREE   DISAGREE   UNDECIDED
7. Natural events such as storms or earthquakes mirror[7] the spiritual and emotional state of humans.
   AGREE   DISAGREE   UNDECIDED
8. The average citizen can be manipulated[8] to do the will of politicians.
   AGREE   DISAGREE   UNDECIDED
9. Money often comes between friends.
   AGREE   DISAGREE   UNDECIDED
10. Ghosts can bring warnings to the living.
    AGREE   DISAGREE   UNDECIDED
11. It is better to commit suicide than be taken prisoner or a slave.
    AGREE   DISAGREE   UNDECIDED
12. Murder can only be avenged[9] with murder.
    AGREE   DISAGREE   UNDECIDED
13. "The laurels of the warrior must at all times be dyed in blood." [10]
    AGREE   DISAGREE   UNDECIDED
14. *Dulce et decorum est pro patria mori.*[11] English translation: "It is sweet and fitting to die for one's country."
    AGREE   DISAGREE   UNDECIDED
15. Flattery will get you anywhere.
    AGREE   DISAGREE   UNDECIDED
16. An honest person is hard to find.
    AGREE   DISAGREE   UNDECIDED
17. A real man is stern, fearless, strong, and tough.
    AGREE   DISAGREE   UNDECIDED
18. In a marriage, your spouse should know all your secrets.
    AGREE   DISAGREE   UNDECIDED

continued on next page

19. When torn between your love for your country and love of a friend, choose your country.
    AGREE   DISAGREE   UNDECIDED
20. The person we most often deceive is ourselves.
    AGREE   DISAGREE   UNDECIDED

Journal Entry—Optional

Choose the statement that most interests you and explore in a journal these questions:

- Why did I answer this statement the way I did?
- How does this statement relate to my life?
- Do others believe differently than I do? Why?
- How does this statement reflect current events or the times we live in?
- What big ideas come from this statement?

1. Assassinate: To kill secretly and suddenly, especially a politician or leader

2. Will: Wishes or desires

3. Heed: Pay attention to

4. Psychic: A person who is sensitive to spiritual and supernatural information and influences

5. Astrologer: A person who predicts the future using the positions of the planets, sun, and moon

6. Ethical: Moral, righteous

7. Mirror: Reflect, imitate, represent

8. Manipulated: Controlled, directed, pushed around

9. Avenge: Punish, retaliate, pay back

10. Laurel: Honor. In ancient Rome, the laurel wreath (a circular wreath worn on the head, made of the laurel evergreen leaves and branches) was used to crown a war commander after a victory. (Reed and Kellogg, qtd in Florey)

11. Horace, Odes iii 2.13

Handout 1.7, What's the Big Idea in *Julius Caesar*? An Interest Inventory

Name _____ Class _____ Date _____

Directions: What big ideas from *Julius Caesar* interest you? Look up words as needed.

1. **Circle your favorite ideas below**. These may interest you because they relate to your life or to favorite books, films, and other works of art.

2. **Choose one idea to discuss**. Explain in the space provided why this idea matters to (a) you right now, and (b) others you know, including world events.

3. **Make word families.** Connect ideas that relate and that are similar.

4. **(Optional) Just for fun.** In the blanks, write new ideas you want to explore.

AMBITION	APPEARANCE	CAPRICE	CHAOS
CONSPIRACY	CONSTANCY	COURAGE	COWARDICE
DECEPTION	DOMINANCE	ENVY	FATE
FEAR	FRAILTY	FREE WILL	GLORY
HEROISM	HONESTY	HONOR	IDEALISM
INGRATITUDE	LEADERSHIP	LOVE	LOYALTY
MANHOOD	MANIPULATION	NATURE	_____
PATRIOTISM	PERSUASION	POWER	REALISM
REVENGE	TRUST	_____	_____

An Important Idea:

Choose one big idea from the list. Why does this idea matter to you, others, and the world?

_____

_____

_____

_____

_____

_____

_____

_____

_____

_____

_____

_____

continued on next page

Word Families:

Which ideas relate?

Word Family (list all ideas that relate)	My Reasoning For Why These Words Relate
Family #1:	
Family #2:	
Family #3:	

Handout 1.8, Digging Up Themes in *Julius Caesar*

Name _____ Class _____ Date _____

Directions: What big ideas from *Julius Caesar* interest you?

1. **Circle your favorite big ideas**. These ideas may interest you because they relate to your life, to history and world events, or to your favorite books, films, and other works of art.

2. **Choose three ideas to convert to essential questions**.

3. **Choose one question to discuss**. Explore in the space provided your answers to one essential question.

4. **(Optional) Just for fun:** Name big ideas not listed that interest you, and predict how a play such as *Julius Caesar* might answer this essential question.

An *essential question* is a question that explores a big idea. It analyzes a conflict or an issue raised by literature like *Julius Caesar*. When you pose an essential question, you search for answers, which are themes, or essential understandings. (In writing, these become thesis statements; some pre-play poll statements, for example, might work as a thesis for an essay.) Here are examples of big ideas that lead to essential questions.

LEADERSHIP: What is the difference between leadership and tyranny?
IDEALISM: How idealistic may a leader be? Should a leader be more of a realist?
MANIPULATION: Can the average citizen be manipulated?
HEROISM: What makes a true hero?
LOVE: Should you love your country more than family or friends?

Choose three ideas to convert to essential questions:

AMBITION	APPEARANCE	CAPRICE	CHAOS
CONSPIRACY	CONSTANCY	COURAGE	COWARDICE
DECEPTION	DOMINANCE	ENVY	FATE
FEAR	FRAILTY	FREE WILL	GLORY
HEROISM	HONESTY	HONOR	IDEALISM
INGRATITUDE	LEADERSHIP	LOVE	LOYALTY
MANHOOD	MANIPULATION	NATURE	_____
PATRIOTISM	PERSUASION	POWER	REALISM
REVENGE	TRUST	_____	_____

continued on next page

Essential question #1: _____
_____
_____
_____

Essential question #2: _____
_____
_____
_____

Essential question #3: _____
_____
_____
_____

Possible answers to essential question # ___: _____
_____
_____
_____
_____
_____
_____
_____
_____
_____

Handout 1.10, Act 1 Quiz

Name_____ Period_____

CLOSED-BOOK SECTION

1. Tribunes Flavius and Murellus send the citizens home because
    a. The carpenter is starting a brawl.[1]
    b. Citizens are dishonoring Pompey by honoring Caesar.
    c. Citizens have displeased Caesar by using cheap decorations.
    d. The carpenter and cobbler make fun of Pompey's battle losses.

2. The soothsayer's[2] prediction to Caesar is:
    a. "Beware of March 15."
    b. "Calpurnia will not bear children."
    c. "Antony, your good-luck charm, will lose the race."
    d. "Beware of lean men who are ambitious."

3. Brutus confesses to Cassius his fear that
    a. Cassius is angry with him.
    b. Antony is not to be trusted.
    c. The people will not accept Caesar as ruler.
    d. The people are choosing Caesar for their king.

4. Cassius tries to convince Brutus
    a. To beware of Casca and Cinna.
    b. To let go of his fears and trust Caesar.
    c. To mistrust Caesar's sudden rise to power and his fitness to be Rome's leader.
    d. To mistrust the Roman citizens, since they are "refuse" and "foolish."

5. Casca reports that
    a. The citizens of Rome stink.
    b. Antony offered a crown to Caesar three times.
    c. Caesar had an epileptic fit.
    d. All of the above
    e. A and B only

6. In the final scene of act 1, all of the following occurs EXCEPT:
    a. Lions walk the streets and slaves' hands are burning with fire.
    b. Casca agrees to support Cassius's plot.
    c. Cicero says people interpret weather however they wish.
    d. Cassius hides his true feelings about Caesar from Casca.

continued on next page

7. Identify the abstract words in the following lines. Circle all that apply.

   Cassius: *I know where I will wear this dagger then:*

   Cassius from bondage will deliver Cassius.

   Therein, ye gods, you make the weak most strong;

   Therein, ye gods, you tyrants do defeat.

8. Pick an abstract word from the passage and list four connotations of this word:

   _____   _____   _____   _____

9. What years did Caesar live?_____

10. When did Shakespeare write *Julius Caesar*?_____

11. What three groups ruled Rome in Caesar's time?
    a) _____   b) _____
    c) _____

OPEN-BOOK SECTION

12. Choose the best noun or adjective to describe the following characters and offer two specific actions, statements, or thoughts from act 1 that proves your characterization is correct.

    a. Caesar: _____ (noun or adjective)
       a. Proof #1: _____
       b. Proof #2: _____
    b. Cassius: _____ (noun or adjective)
       a. Proof #1: _____
       b. Proof #2: _____
    c. Brutus: _____ (noun or adjective)
       a. Proof #1: _____
       b. Proof #2: _____

13. Write a "satisfying sandwich" paragraph (topic sentence, context, supporting details, and commentary) in response to either question:

    a. *Characterization:* Which character seems most likely to be the hero of the story right now: Julius Caesar, Brutus, Cassius, or Antony? Why?

    b. *Big ideas:* Which of these ideas seems the most important based on what you know so far about characters and events—conspiracy, envy, glory, fear, or ingratitude? Why?

1. Brawl: Fight

2. Soothsayer: Fortuneteller, psychic

Handout 1.12, Compacting Fun: Suggested Activities and Projects

Before you begin working, we will need to discuss:

- Which assignments should be completed;
- Your schedule to complete assignments; and
- Rubrics for evaluating your work.

Short-Term Projects

1. *In-depth journaling.* Complete dialectical journals for selected scenes. Identify key words and big ideas, pose essential questions, and discover essential understandings. Search for figurative language, motifs, symbols, emphasis created by iambic pentameter, and other rhythmic elements that prove essential understandings. Deliver journals in an old-school format (bound like a folio of Shakespeare plays, and research how these were composed and published) or in a new-school format (as a blog).

2. *Research it and teach it.* Research one or more of the following topics and present information to the class in a mini-lesson of twenty minutes using slideshow, film clips, acting, recitation, demonstration, models, etc. Or create an interactive Web space where students can come to learn about your research. Make your presentation, whether live or virtual, engaging for your classmates. Research (a) Aristotle's definition of *tragedy* and Shakespeare's five-act structure; (b) Plutarch's *Lives* and the biography of Caesar; (c) daily life in London (late 1500s and early 1600s; even though the play is set in ancient Rome, characters reflect some Elizabethan culture); (d) the Roman Republic and politics in Caesar's time; (e) Roman religious beliefs (including the feast of Lupercal and astrology); and (f) Roman warfare, the life of soldiers, and beliefs about honor and suicide.

3. *Character profile: The making of a murderer.* Several characters commit murder in this play. Profile one of them in the spirit of police detective work and build a psychological portrait to understand character motivation and traits. Examine Cassius, Brutus, or Casca. Write (a) an essay with a wanted poster that explains to the public who these characters are, their motivations, and why they are wanted; (b) a prosecutorial speech condemning their actions, outlining the murderers' motives, and analyzing the depravity of their actions; or (c) a prison interview between a psychologist and the character identifying his motivations and traits. Bonus: research criminal profiling and the career of criminal psychology, and apply what you learn to this project.

4. *Epigrammatic endeavors: Characters as one-line poems.* Poet Michael McFee explains that the one-line poem "resists elaboration and keeps rounding itself down to a single line, [and is] one that takes hours or days or months or years to achieve just the right shape. The inspiration-irritation yields a single pearl" (66). He quotes a one-line poem by William Matthews, its title borrowed from *Hamlet*:

continued on next page

To Thine Own Self Be True
As if you had a choice.

Pick three to five characters from *Julius Caesar* and write one-line poems for them. Choose a phrase that the character says (or that is said about the character) as the title. Follow that title with a pithy, intense line of "witty soulful brevity" (McFee 66). Create a poetry chapbook or website, and consider performing your work and leading your classmates in a poetry-making exercise.

Long-Term Projects

1. *Caesar the whole person.* Use encyclopedias and historical references, such as Plutarch's *Lives*, to learn more about the character of Caesar. Then examine the play and find as many quotations as possible that list Caesar's strengths and flaws. Create a poster that illustrates both and prepare an essay or an oral presentation that answers these essential questions: How flawed was Caesar? How serious are these flaws when considering someone for leadership? How much should we trust what the senators say in the play vis-à-vis recorded history? You should also study and reference other great leaders, such as Abraham Lincoln, who were paradoxical in their beliefs, leadership, and choices. See the *Newsweek* article, "The Man Who Made Us Whole" by Christopher Hitchens, for a discussion of the complexity of our heroes.

2. *Motif tracker.* Certain motifs recur in Shakespeare plays: names, oaths (swearing), day/night, clothing, and ghosts. Read another history play, such as *Richard III, Henry V,* or *Macbeth,* and write an essay, prepare a chart, or build a slide show or interactive website that compares the use of two or more motifs. Answer these essential questions: What role do motifs play in plot and character development? How are these motifs used similarly and differently? What big ideas and themes (essential understandings) do these motifs express? (Pay close attention to ambition, leadership, conspiracy, etc.)

3. *Junior version of Julius Caesar.* Present a 15-minute version of the play or one scene reduced to its core elements. Identify the themes that to you define the play and then select those moments and scenes that best represent and render the themes. Use the cut script models and student scenes for *Romeo and Juliet* and other plays found at the following website, http://www.mainelyshakespeare.com/cutscripts.html and http://mainelyshakespeare.com/sceneofmonth.html, to direct your editing choices. Choose an audience that would most appreciate a 15-minute version of the play: your class, younger students, parents, school community, etc. You can work with other compacting students to present the play. Make your choices of acting and blocking, costumes, scenery, music, and other features demonstrate themes. If you are very ambitious, film the process and build a website with links to video showing the stages of creating this work.

continued on next page

4. *Julius Caesar, the new bestseller.* Rewrite *Julius Caesar* as a novella or a short story. Make intentional choices about point of view with the help of fiction writing guides, such as *Shaping the Story* or *A Writer's Guide to Fiction*. Will it be omniscient, third-person discerning, third-person limited, second person, first person, or a mix of point of views? Where will you include scenes with dialogue, and where will scene be changed to summary? How will the new point(s) of view affect scene and summary? How will you describe character, setting, and action? Make a plot map or outline, decide which characters will tell this story, and complete multiple drafts. You can keep your work more private and submit only to the teacher or launch the work as a "wovel" (Web novel).

5. *Julius Caesar as fanfiction.* Using the same principles described in #4, write the scenes after act 5, before act 5, or "between the acts," to show characters from other angles.

6. *Letters to a senator.* Write a series of letters addressed to various modern political leaders explaining what lessons they might learn from the play. Explain big ideas, essential questions, and essential understandings the play explores and how these ideas apply to modern political, diplomatic, and social problems leaders must address. Conduct research to make insightful connections between literature and modern events. Present your work in a display that is an interactive learning center or website.

7. *The* Julius Caesar *Guide to Leadership.* Did you know some business and government training programs use Shakespeare plays? Read "Friends, Generals and Captains of Industry, Lend Me Your Ears" at *The New York Times* (visit http://www.nytimes.com/2005/01/31/theater/31shak.html?pagewanted=print&position) and then return to *Julius Caesar* to seek advice for leaders. Use passages from the play to develop a training manual (print or electronic) for a particular profession or leaders in general. Provide your advice and interpretations based on the play's wisdom.

8. *Oratorical explorations.* Study several examples of great oratory from American history, such as Abraham Lincoln's speeches and Dr. Martin Luther King, Jr.'s speeches. Identify the rhetorical devices—many of them derived from ancient Roman oratory—that make each speech persuasive, powerful, and memorable. Take Antony's famous speech from act 3 and draw comparisons. Create a speechmaker's manual that teaches the art of rhetoric and references great speeches. Teach your classmates with demonstrations and explications of rhetoric. Bonus: work with a speech society member, such as Toastmaster's, to learn more about the art of public speaking.

continued on next page

9. *Cinematic study.* Watch the Burge and Mankiewicz film versions of *Julius Caesar* and compare key scenes in terms of camera angles, length of shots, lighting, sound track/sound effects, and screenplay. After detailing their similarities and differences, argue for effectiveness of directorial/editorial choices in characterization and plot development, using either an essay or a live or Web presentation including film clips.

10. *Film it.* Storyboard and/or write the screenplay for a modern or other historical setting for a version of *Julius Caesar*. Pick a few key scenes to storyboard or write out in detail. Which historical setting and actors would make the best version? Present in poster, graphic novel, or Web format.

11. *College-level study.* Develop a list of questions about characterization, events, themes, and diction. Then, with mentor assistance, contact a university literature professor or a local community expert such as a theater director for an interview to further probe and discuss the play. If you have permission, film the interview, and edit as a documentary that tracks your pursuit of your questions.

12. *Workshop it.* Attend a professional production of a Shakespeare play. With mentor assistance, set up an interview with the direction, dramaturg, and/or actors, and come prepared with thorough questions so you can direct a scene from *Julius Caesar*. Find volunteers to develop a scene with you and present to the class.

13. *Shakespeare the man.* Read Bill Bryson's book, *Shakespeare: The World as Stage*, and develop a list of research questions. Investigate an aspect of Shakespeare's life and present your findings in an essay, museum display, or "living history" speech (you playing William Shakespeare).

Lesson 3: Tips for Tackling Translation

Reading Skills (50 to 90 minutes)

Begin with a WCA reading skills mini-lesson, then place students in TR groups for CR analysis while you give assistance. End class with groups reporting back in a WCA.

> This prereading lesson helps students learn skills of diction analysis that are key to translation and annotation.

At the end of the prereading lesson, the students will know:

- the difference between concrete and abstract words (AS)
- the definition of connotation and key words (AS)
- the definition of annotation (AS)
- tips for tackling translation (AS)
- the definition of essential questions (OT/ADV)

Students will be able to:

- use three or more translation strategies—in particular, Guess the Meaning, Get the Point, and Build a Family—as part of annotation (AS)
- create word families (AS)
- ask essential questions (OT/ADV)

Students will understand:

- active reading of Shakespeare requires multiple, thoughtful steps (AS)
- translation strategies unlock the treasure of Shakespeare's language (AS)

Students will explore this question:

- How can we translate Shakespeare's language? (AS)

Materials and Handouts

Use the following handouts and materials during this lesson. Most appear at the end of the lesson (page 42) unless otherwise noted to be at the companion website.

- Handout 1.13, Tips for Tackling the Translation; Handout 1.14, Figure Out Flavius; Handout 1.15-A and B, Figure Out Cassius.
- Dictionaries and glossaries
- Quotations posted in large text that you and students can mark up, with multicolored markers or sticky notes available: Antony: *"Friends, Romans, countrymen, lend me your ears;/I come to bury Caesar, not to praise him,"* and *"When that the poor have cried, Caesar hath wept: Ambition should be made of sterner stuff."*

Companion Website

See http://www.lynhawks.com for the following materials:

- Handout 1.6, Recitation Regulars
- Handout 1.16, Finding the Complete Thought Mini-Lesson
- Handout 1.17, Antony's Speech

Activities

STEP 1. WCA: Homework Check-In, Mini-Lesson, and Recitation Regulars (20 minutes)

1. Ask TQs about homework from Handout 1.7, What's the Big Idea in *Julius Caesar*? An Interest Inventory and Handout 1.8, Digging Up Themes in *Julius Caesar*.

   a. ELL/NOV: What are word families? What big ideas link to word families?

   b. OT/ADV: What is an essential question? What questions do these big ideas inspire for you?

   c. ADV: What's the difference between a big idea and a theme (EU)?

By asking TQs, you allow everyone the opportunity to be an expert and teach one another. Use homework review to clarify terms, such as concrete, abstract, and big ideas.

---

2. Explain that today students will begin learning strategies for tackling Shakespeare's language. His language is a treasure chest locked up by 400-year-old diction and syntax. One can get at the gold with translation strategies. Ask students to read aloud the first part of Antony's statement—*"When that the poor have cried, Caesar hath wept. . . ."*

   a. Ask students to flag the first unfamiliar word needing translation. They will point to "hath." Ask students to "build on what you know" and "guess the meaning." How did they decide what "hath" means? Discuss the use of context.

b. Ask someone to "consult the experts" and look up the formal definition. Are they correct? Ask someone to restate the quotation in modern language, such as, "When the poor have cried, Caesar wept," or "Caesar wept when the poor cried."

c. Repeat the process (defining and restating), using " . . . *Ambition should be made of sterner stuff.*" Keep discussion to direct translation rather than interpretation.

d. Introduce the "get the point" strategy to search for key words. Key words belong to word families, connect to big ideas, and inspire questions.

e. Ask students to read aloud the quotation once more and ask students to identify key words. They should flag *poor, cried, Caesar, wept, ambition, sterner,* and *stuff.* Ask which are abstract nouns, noting that abstract nouns are helpful key words. Circle *ambition, stuff,* and *poor.*

Some might argue that *stuff* and *the poor* are rather abstract, which is correct. Yet poverty doesn't feel abstract to the poor. Degrees of abstraction depend on perspective and context. *Stuff* is a most abstract noun and least helpful when identifying key words leading to big ideas.

---

f. Ask students which words seem most important or most key. Tell students that in order to select, they must see which words build the best word families. Demonstrate with a visual how to find connotation by webbing lines from the word *Caesar* and asking them for the first suggestions that come to mind—words such as *leader, powerful, name of play, Rome*; from *ambition* (*power, glory, desire, climbing*); and from *sterner* (*harder, tougher, firmer, colder*). Explain how *Caesar, ambition,* and *sterner* are "key" because of their resonance—the ability to build word families.

g. Explain that you just "built a family" using connotations, which are synonyms and associations with the original word, sometimes suggestive of big ideas. Explain that by marking up the quotation, you are modeling annotation.

h. TQ, ADV: Ask someone to reread Antony's quotation and state how Antony himself raises essential questions for the play. Shakespeare allows for exciting ambiguity, demonstrating the complexity of his very human characters: Was Caesar too ambitious? Was Caesar a hero or a tyrant? Was Caesar too frail? Was Caesar too kind to lead?

If possible, make Handout 1.6, Recitation Regulars, available in a learning center. This can be a place for student folders, recitation practice, and other anchoring activities.

---

3. Explain procedures for recitation regulars, an anchoring activity. Students can return to it when they finish class work early. You will pull one or more names from a hat daily for recitations. Today, guess what? The name happens to be the teacher's! Demonstrate what you expect from recitation regulars by reciting at least six to ten lines of verse. Ask students to keep two elements in mind while you recite: (a) what are the key words? and (b) what praise and constructive criticism might they offer you?

Depending on class chemistry and supportiveness, you may prefer that recitations happen in private conference or small groups rather than as a WCA. You can also limit recitations to four lines. During any presentation, insist on a supportive audience in which students offer meaningful compliments and constructive directorial help.

STEP 2. WCA, MR Pairs, and WCA: Tips for Tackling the Language (30 to 60 minutes)

1. Distribute Handout 1.13, Tips for Tackling the Translation, page 42, and explain that these are the go-to strategies for translating and reading the play. They will use this handout throughout the unit. Have students read the tips aloud.

2. Optional: Demonstrate Tip #1 using a famous quotation from the play. Ask students to try "Get the Structure" on "*Friends, Romans, countrymen, lend me your ears; I come to bury Caesar, not to praise him*" (act 3, scene 2). How many sentences, or complete thoughts, can they find? Where are the subject and the predicate? Identify the word where each complete thought ends.

3. Distribute CR Handout 1.14, Figure Out Flavius, page 43. Explain the context, including Flavius and Murellus's great anger at the citizens for their short memories of Pompey. Read the passage aloud for students.

4. Ask students to find a TR or MR partner to complete the analysis using Handout 1.13.

   a. Let students know where resources, such as dictionaries, are available.

   b. Tell students if they finish early, they can prepare for recitation regulars.

Establish rules for how and when students move to anchoring activities. Anchoring activities are part of good choices a student makes when he or she finishes work early or is stumped on a particular task. Maintain classroom folders and areas of the room where students can access needed materials. See Diane Heacox's *Differentiating Instruction in the Regular Classroom* for classroom management tips for rules and rituals.

---

5. Ask students to report to the whole class their translations. Ask: which tips were easiest or hardest to follow? Why? Which ones are most helpful? Begin a metacognitive process of self-assessment so students can gauge their readiness and choose those tips that most help them improve their skills and understanding.

Homework Options

1. Ask students to complete CR Handout 1.15A or B. Explain:

   a. The context: Cassius is not impressed with Caesar due to a perceived frailty—that Caesar, a war commander, had a bout of sickness.

   b. Homework as pretest: Explain that this homework is practice for an upcoming pretest to identify their prior knowledge and skill in translating a passage. Your job is to provide appropriate challenge throughout the unit. Students should choose B if they want greater challenge. Both will receive the same amount of straight credit.

The TR homework translation exercises prepare students for the upcoming pretest, Handout 1.18, Make Sense of Murellus. The choose A or B option helps you not only gauge student readiness and interest but also motivation. Who gravitates toward challenge when there is no grade reward?

2. Other options:

   a. Ask compacting applicants to prepare for their pretests.

   b. Ask students to choose and practice a passage for recitation regulars.

   c. Give the character analysis pretest.

   d. Ask students to do an artistic, symbolic rendering of the ten tips for tackling translation. They can create ten symbols on an index card, bookmark, or electronic document as a reminder and quick guide while reading. Lead a brainstorming session to generate ideas. "Sound it out" might be rendered as a volume icon, and "consult the experts" as the image of a book, and so forth.

   e. Give a creative writing assignment. Prompt #1: Write a poem sharing your life's ambitions, called "I Dream, I Aim." Prompt #2: Write a dialogue between you and someone you know in which you (or the other person) make an accusation of weakness. What frailty is the basis of the accusation?

Notes on Differentiation

1. To more fully explain annotation, consider having students read excerpts of Mortimer Adler's essay "How to Mark a Book." He offers a coding system to aid active reading, such as underlining, starring, and circling.

2. If many of your students struggle with grammar, review terms of *subject, predicate, verb,* (and *independent* and *dependent clause* if students can't spot fragments), and teach the Finding the Complete Thought Mini-Lesson (Handout 1.16, available at http://www.lynhawks.com)—a script for a 30-minute minilesson.

Tweet for translation! If you are willing to maintain a Twitter page, create a translation tweet site. Every week post two lines of text from the play that class or CRs will not review, and award bonus points for each student who brings a translation to you that uses one or more tips to translate. For students without Internet access, post these same tweets on your board weekly.

---

3. The TR homework (CR Handout 1.15A or B) prepares students for the upcoming pretest, Handout 1.18, Make Sense of Murellus, page 49.

a. You may choose to give Tier A to ELL and NOV students so they can continue to practice word families and key words and demonstrate whether they understand the details of Caesar's sickness. (He has a fever, shakes with "fit," and turns pale.)

b. You can give Tier B to OT and ADV so they can experience translating slightly more text and try a higher-level question that gets at Cassius' obsession with Caesar's sickness and leads to a greater understanding of big ideas, such as *envy, frailty, leadership,* and *manhood.* ADV students may be able to elicit essential questions such as *Is Caesar too frail to lead? Is Cassius demanding too much of his leader? Is it unmanly to succumb to sickness? Is Cassius a dangerous person?*

Handout 1.13, Tips for Tackling the Translation

1. **GET THE STRUCTURE:**
   a. Where is the subject?
   b. Where is the predicate?
   c. Where does the complete thought end?

2. **SOUND IT OUT:** What modern word does this word sound like?

3. **BUILD ON WHAT YOU KNOW:** How can words you understand help you clarify words you don't?

4. **GUESS THE MEANING:** What are your guesses at definitions?

5. **CONSULT THE EXPERTS:** What does the dictionary, thesaurus, or text reference say?

6. **SKIP FOR NOW:** What words can you put aside for now?

7. **GET THE JOKE:** What puns made Elizabethans laugh? Cultural references?

8. **GET THE POINT:** What are the key words?

9. **BUILD A FAMILY:** What word families (synonyms and connotations) come from key words?

10. **NAME THAT THEME:** What big ideas appear in this passage? What essential understandings or themes?

CR Handout 1.14, Figure Out Flavius. Act 1, Scene 1

Directions: Annotate and translate using Handout 1.13, Tips for Tackling the Language.

Background: Flavius is a Roman tribune, a nobleman who serves in the military. He keeps order in the streets and reproaches[1] workmen who are not wearing their proper work clothes.

TEXT	ANNOTATION/TRANSLATION

Hence[2]! Home, you idle creatures, get you home!

Is this a holiday? What, know you not,

Being mechanical[3], you ought not to walk

Upon a labouring day without the sign

Of your profession[4]? Speak, what trade art thou[5]?

_____

_____

_____

_____

_____

Key words: _____
_____

Word families: _____
_____

(Optional) Big ideas and essential questions: _____
_____

1. Reproaches: Criticizes, condemns
2. Hence: Go away, get out of here!
3. Mechanical: Manual laborers, people who work with their hands
4. Sign of your profession: Work clothes and tools. Sumptuary laws demanded people dress a certain way to show class distinctions (Seccara)
5. Thou: The familiar form of "you," used when a nobleman spoke to someone of a lower class

Teaching Julius Caesar: *A Differentiated Approach* © 2010 Lyn Fairchild Hawks.

CR Handout 1.15A, Figure Out Cassius. Act 1, Scene 2.

Directions: Annotate and translate using Handout 1.13, Tips for Tackling the Translation.

Background: Cassius, a nobleman and a senator, is describing a time when he saw Caesar sick.

TEXT   ANNOTATION/TRANSLATION

He had a fever when he was in Spain,

And when the fit[1] was on him I did mark[2]

How he did shake. 'Tis[3] true, this god did shake,

His coward lips did from their colour fly,

And that same eye whose bend[4] doth awe the world

Did lose his lustre.[5]

_____

_____

_____

_____

_____

Key words: _____

Word families: _____

What happens when Caesar gets sick?_____

(Optional) Big ideas and essential questions: _____

1. Fit: An epileptic fit. Caesar suffered from epilepsy
2. Mark: See
3. 'Tis: Abbreviation for "it is"
4. Bend: Glance, look
5. Lustre: Another spelling for "luster"

Teaching Julius Caesar: *A Differentiated Approach* © 2010 Lyn Fairchild Hawks.

Handout 1.15B, Figure Out Cassius. Act 1, Scene 2.

Directions: Annotate and translate using Handout 1.13, Tips for Tackling the Translation.

Background: Cassius, a nobleman and a senator, is describing a time when he saw Caesar sick.

TEXT	ANNOTATION/TRANSLATION

He had a fever when he was in Spain,

And when the fit[1] was on him I did mark[2]

How he did shake. 'Tis true, this god did shake,

His coward lips did from their colour fly,

And that same eye whose bend[3] doth awe the world

Did lose his lustre.[4] I did hear him groan,

Ay,[5] and that tongue of his that bade the Romans

Mark him and write his speeches in their books,

'Alas,' it cried, 'give me some drink, Titinius,'[6]

As a sick girl.

Key words: _____

Why do you think Cassius is so interested in Caesar's sickness? Why does it matter?

_____

Essential questions: _____

1. Fit: An epileptic fit. Caesar suffered from epilepsy
2. Mark: See
3. Bend: Glance, look
4. Lustre: Another spelling for "luster"
5. Ay: Yes
6. Titinius: A friend of Caesar's

Teaching Julius Caesar: *A Differentiated Approach* © 2010 Lyn Fairchild Hawks.

Lesson 4: Show What You Know

Assessment (50 minutes)

Give a pretest to AS.

This pretest will help you see what students already know and can do when it comes to annotation and translation of passages from Shakespeare.

At the end of the pretest, students will know:

- the definition of annotation (AS)
- tips for tackling translation (AS)

Students will be able to:

- practice two or more tips for tackling translation as part of annotation (AS)

Students will understand:

- pretests help a teacher diagnose what students already know and can do so the teacher can provide an appropriate level of challenge (AS)
- we all bring prior knowledge and experience to a Shakespeare play (AS)

Students will explore this question:

- How do we translate Shakespeare's language? (AS)

Materials and Handouts

Use the following handouts and materials during this lesson. Most appear at the end of the lesson (page 49) unless otherwise noted to be at the companion website.

- Handout 1.13, Tips for Tackling the Translation; Handout 1.18, Pretest: Make Sense of Murellus; and Handout 1.19, Act 1 Journals.
- Dictionaries and glossaries, one per student (if possible).

Activities

STEP 1. WCA: Recitation Regulars and Pretest Setup (10 minutes)

1. Ask students to get out Handout 1.13, Tips for Tackling Transla-

tion. Ask which tips students found to be most helpful when completing the homework of CRs 1.15A–B.

2. Pull a name from the hat and invite the first student to perform in recitation regulars. (You might ask students who are least shy or the most gifted at public speaking to go first.) Using the rubric on Handout 1.6, Recitation Regulars, available at http://www.lynhawks.com, model effective feedback: specific compliments and constructive criticism that directly reference rubric criteria.

3. Explain the purpose of this pretest: for students to demonstrate prior plot knowledge and translation skills. Pretests also help a teacher provide an appropriate amount of challenge for each student. With sincere effort, everyone can earn straight credit.

If students ask how you use test results, explain you design certain assignments to match different skills and interests. Tell them test results are also temporary, snapshots in time to be taken again.

---

4. Give two dramatic readings of Murellus's speech, the first without the handout in their hands. The second time, distribute Handout 1.18, Pretest: Make Sense of Murellus, and ask them to read along with you.

5. Tell students to work independently on this test. If they seek help from others, you will not have an accurate reading on their prior knowledge and skill. They may use dictionaries and Handout 1.13, Tips for Tackling the Language.

STEP 2. WCA: Pretest (30 to 40 minutes)

1. Give thirty minutes or more for this preassessment. Compacting applicants can take quizzes for act 1 through act 5 and/ or the translation test (Handout 1.9 available at http://www. lynhawks.com). You may wish to send compacting applicants to another area for testing.

2. Circulate to encourage students to use resources: dictionaries, glossaries, Handout 1.13.

3. Collect work after thirty minutes. Ask: Which translation tips were most helpful this time?

Homework Options

1. Ask students to complete a journal about a big idea of interest to them (see Handout 1.19, Act 1 Journals).

2. Give a creative writing assignment. Prompt #1: Write a dialogue/skit about disrespect, in which a group of people are being disrespectful and someone challenges them. Prompt #2: Write a scene in which one person convinces another to plot against someone else. Prompt #3: Write a scene in which someone experiences great popularity and success and three other people gossip about that person. Prompt #4: Write a scene in which strange, horrible natural events occur, and two people discuss their superstitions and concerns about them.

Notes on Differentiation

1. *Assessment of Pretests:* Sort your students' pretests to determine future TR groups.

   a. ELL and NOV readers are those who can translate a few words and phrases correctly, and/or can list a few or no plot events.

   b. OT readers know a few plot events and/or are able to translate some lines with 30 to 50 percent accuracy.

   c. ADV readers know several plot events and/or can translate 60 percent or more accurately.

   d. Vary percentages as needed depending on your students' age, readiness, etc.

2. Consider asking a few students at varying readiness levels for informal feedback about how they felt about their performance. Continue to inquire about various assignments and assessments as part of your ongoing research throughout the unit.

Handout 1.18, Pretest: Make Sense of Murellus

Student Name _____ Period _____

Try your best. This survey helps me assess your needs as a learner. Stop whenever time is called.

I. **Past Experience:** Have you read, seen the play or movies of, or ever acted in *Julius Caesar*? If yes, please explain below. If no, skip to the next question.

❏ Yes _____

_____

II. **Plot Knowledge:** List as many events as you know occur in the story of *Julius Caesar*.

1. _____
2. _____
3. _____
4. _____
5. _____
6. _____
7. _____
8. _____
9. _____
10. _____

III. **Language Translation:** Write your translation of each line on the next page. You do not have to translate word-for-word. Or, if you don't know many words, write synonyms for the words you do know. You may use your Tips for Tackling the Translation handout and a dictionary.

Background: Murellus is a Roman tribune helping Flavius keep order in the streets where workmen celebrate because Caesar won a civil war against his co-ruler, Pompey.

TEXT	ANNOTATION /TRANSLATION

You blocks, you stones, you worse than senseless things!

O you hard hearts, you cruel men of Rome,

Knew you not Pompey? Many a time and oft[1]

Have you climb'd up to walls and battlements,

To towers and windows, yea, to chimney tops,

continued on next page

Your infants in your arms, and there have sat

The livelong[2] day, with patient expectation,

To see great Pompey pass the streets of Rome

. . . And do you now put on your best attire?[3]

And do you now cull[4] out a holiday?

And do you now strew flowers in his way,

That comes in triumph over Pompey's blood?

Be gone!

Run to your houses, fall upon your knees,

Pray to the gods to intermit[5] the plague

That needs must light on[6] this ingratitude.

1. Oft: Often
2. Livelong: Whole
3. Attire: Clothing
4. Cull: Make into, choose
5. Intermit: Delay
6. "That needs must light on"—that is deserved for

Handout 1.19, Act 1 Journals

Big ideas: caprice, glory, loyalty, leadership, power, deception, frailty, ingratitude

Directions:

1. Write at least 100 words in response to your chosen question.
2. Ask questions and draw conclusions.
3. Give specific examples, such as anecdotes,[1] current events, or allusions.[2]
4. Do not worry about organization, spelling, grammar, or punctuation.

Caprice: Have someone else's feelings for you ever changed very quickly from love to hate or love to apathy?[3] How did it happen? How do you explain it? Have your feelings ever changed that quickly?

Glory: Are there reasons for a person to deserve glory? What form should glory take? Do you agree or disagree with this quotation from Prince Talleyrand: "Love of glory can only create a great hero; contempt of glory creates a great man"?

Loyalty:

Option 1: To whom or what are you extremely loyal? Why?

Option 2: Pick one of these quotations and explain why you agree or disagree.

- Seneca:[4] *Fides sanctissimum humani pectoris bonum est* (*Loyalty is the holiest good in the human heart.*)
- Pandit Nehru:[5] "No policy or maneuver[6] can ever be a right one if it involves the forsaking[7] of a colleague."
- Cambridge Five:[8] "If we ever have to choose between betraying our country or a friend, may God grant us the courage to betray our country."

Leadership: What qualities make a great leader? Who is a great leader whom you admire?

Patriotism: Do you love this country or perhaps another country and profess[10] great loyalty to it? Why or why not?

Power: Should some people in society be given more power than others? Why?

Deception: Have you ever argued yourself into doing something you knew was wrong? Have you ever convinced someone else to do something that was wrong by telling a lie or exaggerating the truth? What happened?

Frailty: What qualities, actions, or choices make a person weak?

Ingratitude: Have you ever been ungrateful or told that you were? Has someone ever been ungrateful to you? What happened?

Challenge Question: Pick any two big ideas and explain what they have in common.

continued on next page

1. Anecdotes: Brief stories from your personal experience or brief stories you have read
2. Allusions: References to well-known individuals and events from history, culture, and the arts
3. Apathy: Lack of interest, emotion, or concern
4. Seneca: A Roman statesman, playwright, and philosopher (4 B.C.–A.D. 65)
5. Nehru: One of the leaders of Indian Independence and India's first prime minister (1889–1964)
6. Maneuver: Strategy or tactic
7. Forsaking: Abandoning or turning away from
8. Cambridge Five: Soviet spies in the United Kingdom during World War II through the 1950s
9. Profess: Declare, swear

Lesson 5: Sneak Preview

Performance and Close Reading (120 minutes)

Begin with a WCA of performance preparation, then move to MR groups in which students practice their scenes. End with a WCA of performance and analysis or CR analysis in TR groups.

> This lesson offers: (a) an acting exercise and prereading activity to help students preview key character motivations and conflicts in the play, and (b) close reading that introduces students to their first line-by-line comprehension activity.

At the end of the lesson, students will know:

- three elements for a compelling plot: motivation, obstacle, and conflict (AS)
- famous quotations from act 1 of *Julius Caesar* (AS)

Students will be able to:

- create a scene that demonstrates character motivations, obstacles, and conflict (AS)

Students will understand:

- drama is based on conflict (AS)

Students will explore this question:

- How do we present a scene with a compelling plot? (AS)

Materials and Handouts

Use the following handouts and materials during this lesson. Most appear at the end of the lesson (page 60) unless otherwise noted to be at the companion website.

- Handout 1.13, Tips for Tackling the Translation; Handout 1.21, Sneak Preview: Scenelet Stretch; Handouts 1.22 A–D, Passing Up Pompey and Celebrating Caesar
- Character List: Julius Caesar, Marcus Brutus, Caius Cassius, Casca, Marc Antony, Octavius Caesar, Calpurnia, Portia, Flavius, and Murellus
- Outline of key events, character motivations, conflicts, and obstacles in act 1, posted in a visible place (see pages 54–55)

- Dictionaries and glossaries
- Box of props and costumes
- Film versions of *Julius Caesar*
- Posted group work guidelines for TR groups, CR analysis (see page 56)

With student help, create a box of props and costumes for performances: scarves and robes for togas; fake daggers made of foil and cardboard, yardsticks, and plastic swords for weaponry; pillows, blankets, plastic buckets, etc. for furniture and scenery, and so forth.

Companion Website

Visit http://www.lynhawks.com for the following handouts:

- Handout 1.20, Anchoring Activities.
- Worst group ever skit and directions.

Activities

STEP 1. WCA: Recitation Regulars and Sneak Preview (20 minutes)

1. Invite a student to perform a recitation. Help students provide effective feedback.
2. Introduce new anchoring activity possibilities. Visit http://www.lynhawks.com for Handout 1.20, Anchoring Activities. If you already have engaging, stand-alone activities for building vocabulary, reviewing parts of speech and topic sentences, etc., make those assignments available at a center for students who finish class work early.

Consider using such sites as FreeRice.com or VocabSushi.com as anchoring activities for vocabulary practice.

---

3. Tell students it's time to get a sneak preview of the play. Ask students to look at the character list and repeat after you the names of all characters. Then review the following outline of act 1, a snapshot of its plot elements, and vocabulary as necessary.
   a. *Scene 1:* Tribunes Flavius and Murellus reprimand Roman citizens because they have forgotten their former ruler,

Pompey, and now celebrate Caesar's victory over him. Tribunes' motivation: anger; obstacle: ignorant citizen behavior; conflict: man versus man, or tribunes versus the citizens.

b. *Scene 2:* A fortuneteller tells Caesar to beware of March 15. Cassius tells Brutus Caesar shouldn't be king. Casca reports Antony offered Caesar the crown three times and the citizens cheered. Cassius and Brutus agree to meet and deliberate over this troubling political situation. Cassius' motivation: jealousy; obstacle: Brutus' caution; conflict: man versus man, or Cassius versus Brutus.

c. *Scene 3:* During a terrible storm full of scary, foreboding signs, Casca and Cassius agree to conspire against Caesar. Motivations: fear, revenge; obstacles: nature, the government of Caesar; conflicts: man versus nature, man versus society, man versus man.

STEP 2. MR Groups: Performance Practice (40 to 50 minutes)

1. Introduce the performance activity by reviewing Handout 1.21, Sneak Preview: Scenelet Stretch, on page 60, with its essential question, "How can we create a scene with a compelling plot?"

a. Review the directions and the rubric, noting:

i. groups should read the first forty lines of the scene at top speed, round-robin style, to dive fearlessly into Shakespeare's language; and

ii. which assessment criteria are required and which are optional.

b. Encourage students to choose groups based on talents.

Early in the unit, post a Help Wanted chart and distribute name tags. Have students stick their names in one or more job columns where they feel qualified to serve: director, actor, costume designer, stage/props manager, musician/sound track engineer, and scenery designer. Use this chart when forming groups.

---

c. Practice should be quick and efficient (40 minutes)

i. Each group should have at least three students. Groups can select a scenelet by pulling a number (1–4) from a hat.

ii. If characters in a scenelet are less than group members, encourage students to creatively involve everyone as narrators, props, and scenery.

          iii. Provide students with props, dictionaries, and glossaries as needed.

    2. If compacting students need more challenge, consider offering a junior version of *Julius Caesar* (Handout 1.12, Compacting Fun, on page 31) instead of this activity.

STEP 3. WCA: Performance and Analysis (30 minutes)

    1. As groups perform scenes, use the rubric from Handout 1.21, Sneak Preview: Scenelet Stretch, to guide the class in giving effective feedback.

    2. TQ, OT/ADV: Explain to students that a theory in psychology says that humans are driven by four main needs: love and belonging, power, freedom, and fun (Glasser). Can characters portrayed in these scenelets represent some of these four needs?

    3. Show act 1, scene 1 from a film version of *Julius Caesar*. TQ, AS: Ask students to identify character motivations, the obstacle(s), and the conflicts.

STEP 4. TR groups: Analysis (30 minutes)

Ask students to work in TR pairs or groups to complete Handouts 1.22A–D, CR: Passing Up Pompey and Celebrating Caesar. Have them follow these guidelines:

CR Group Work Guidelines

- *Facilitator*: Reads directions and keeps the group on task. Leads the discussion about what symbol should be used (see Symbolist role).

- *Reader*: Reads the text aloud, stopping when the Explicator asks.

- *Explicator*: Leads group in translating the lines, stopping the Reader every few lines. Everyone should assist the Explicator, using Handout 1.13, Tips for Tackling the Translation.

- *Researcher*: Uses the book references, a dictionary, or a glossary to define words that the whole group does not know. Everyone should assist the Researcher.

- *Symbolist*: Designs an easy-to-draw symbol that will help everyone remember the events of the plot up to a certain line. (This role is recommended for ELL/NOV groups.)

- *Summarizer*: Leads the discussion about what summary should represent the plot. Creates a list of words, a brief phrase, or even a topic sentence to summarize the group's agreement. (This role is recommended for OT/ADV groups.)

Directions
You will need Handout 1.13, Tips for Tackling the Translation.

1. Choose group roles.

2. Open your books to the scene on your CR. You will need the references in the text.

3. Listen to the Reader read the first five lines of text on this handout.

4. Help the Explicator translate and help the Researcher investigate references.

5. Participate as the Facilitator leads a discussion to propose a symbol for the first five lines or the Summarizer provides a phrase or topic sentence.

6. Copy what the Symbolist draws or what the Summarizer writes.

Proceed through the rest of the text in this manner, explicating and drawing/writing after every few lines.

If your class has several ELL/NOV students, give ample class time to supervise CR work. Post CR group work guidelines and review as needed. You may also want to rehearse your expectations and prevent group meltdowns by acting out a "worst group ever" skit. Visit http://www.lynhawks.com.

Homework Options

- Assign reading of act 1, scene 1. Ask students to read the whole scene and complete Handout 1.22 A, B, C, or D. Assign A to ELLs, B to NOV students, C to OT students, and D to ADV students.

- Or, have students complete these CRs and read the rest of the scene aloud in class the following day. Assign Handout 1.19, Act 1 Journals (51) or creative writing assignment options (pages 21, 40, and 48).

Notes on Differentiation

1. *MR Groups for Scenelet Stretch:* If you haven't already, establish group work standards, preferably with students' help. Keep these standards as a visible contract in the classroom. Use the worst group ever skit (http://www.lynhawks.com) to communicate expectations. As you circulate during group work, help

students keep in mind that "ABC" is crucial, and compliment students and groups who support these goals:

    a. A = All participate;

    b. B = Build on everyone's strengths; and

    c. C = Create consensus.

2. *Tiering the Scenelet Stretch:* Scenelets 2 and 3 require students to juggle multiple motivations, so you may wish to give extra support to groups that pull these numbers, or, if you prefer to tier groups for this activity, give 2 and 3 to more OT/ADV readers.

3. *TR Pairs or Groups for CR Work:* If your students have trouble working in CR groups of three or four, consider placing students in pairs and asking each student to play two roles. For example, one partner can be Reader and Explicator, while the other is Researcher and Symbolist/Summarizer.

4. *CRs:* Select those questions you find most essential for your students, and don't feel obligated to give an entire CR for homework or classwork. The questions on each CR can be split between two periods or between classwork and homework.

Note how CR activities prep students for more intensive writing later, asking them to develop topical subgroups for topic sentences and to gather evidence.

---

5. *Homework:* With your first reading assignment, you have several options.

    a. Assign only a CR rather than independent reading of act 1 if you are concerned about student readiness, or give some students independent reading and others only the CR. The CRs give students a recognizable passage to translate (the same passage from Handout 1.18, Pretest) while asking students to analyze characterization and plot at varying readiness levels. See page 91, Designing CRs, for more information about scaffolding reading questions.

    b. If you decide to assign more reading than the CR, consider giving ELL/NOV students no extra reading, OT students ten to twenty additional lines, and ADV the same amount as OT. If one or more students are profoundly gifted readers, assign them the entire scene.

    c. If you aren't ready to tier assignments, allow students to choose their level. Explain that all levels are challenging, with C and D the toughest. Note which levels students choose. Are they challenging themselves too little or too much? See Grading in a Differentiated Classroom (pages 209–211) for more information about handling TR assignments.

Alternate Approach to Lesson 5

Heard Off Stage. Try this activity instead of the WCA performance activity.

- Ask students with strong acting skills to prepare scene 2 in which Casca reports Caesar's crowning, playing it "live" as it might have happened. Characters needed: Marc Antony, Caesar, and the citizens. Students can use Casca's quotations and improvise the rest of the lines.
- Lead a WCA discussion with TR questions:
  - OT: What is verifiable in the text versus Casca's reporting and interpretation? (We hear shouts, etc., yet . . . did it really happen as Casca says?)
  - AS: How does this scene show us what the Roman citizens think of Caesar?
  - ADV: Why do you think Shakespeare didn't make this a live scene?
  - OT: Does Casca's reporting rather than a live scene cast doubt as to how things happened?
  - ADV: What big ideas does this scene raise?

Shakespeak. Prepare students for Shakespeare's vocabulary by reviewing stage directions and high-frequency archaic words prior to any reading. See *Reading Shakespeare with Young Adults* by Mary Ellen Dakin for lists of words to convert to handouts. Dakin recommends charting high-frequency words to increase fluency and allow the fun of wordplay (13, 18).

1. Find words from act 1 that students will see often in the play.
2. Place them in a chart with columns designated for subjects and objects, predicates, modifiers/phrases/clauses, interjections, and compound adjectives (Dakin).
3. Ask students to create their own sentences using these words.

Handout 1.21, Sneak Preview: Scenelet Stretch Activity

A plot includes three elements:

- Distinct character motivations;
- An obstacle; and
- A conflict.

Two or more characters each want something (**motivations** or goals), but there is an **obstacle** in the way, so, suddenly, you have a **conflict**.

Directions:

1. Read the description of your scenelet from this handout.

2. Find the scenelet in act 1 of your play, and read aloud the first forty lines round-robin style. Aim for quick pickup of lines and speed to get comfortable with the language. Don't worry about understanding anything more than the plot summary on this handout.

3. Create a scenelet of two to four minutes demonstrating three elements of the rubric.

4. Find three lines from the text to speak in your scene. The rest can be in modern English.

5. Practice several times. Involve everyone in the final performance.

Rubric

Participation: All group members are involved with meaningful roles. YES NO (required)

Scene demonstrates character motivations, obstacle, and conflict
YES NO (required)
(Character motivations are clear; obstacle blocks characters from goals; tension results.)

Choose one additional criterion from the following list:

Pronunciation, clarity, volume	novice	on-target	advanced
Emphasis, intensity, dramatic effect	novice	on-target	advanced
Creativity: Humor, use of props, etc.	novice	on-target	advanced

Scenelet 1: Stop the Disrespect. Act 1, scene 1.

- **Characters and Motivations:** Flavius and Murellus, tribunes who want Pompey to be respected; cobbler and carpenter, citizens who want to party because Caesar won a war.

- **Obstacles:** For Flavius and Murellus, Caesar's success and the citizens' ignorance; for the cobbler and carpenter, Flavius and Murellus.

- **Conflict:** Flavius and Murellus *versus*[1] the people and Caesar.

continued on next page

- **Consequences:** Flavius and Murellus accuse the cobbler and carpenter of disrespect; they tear down the decorations in honor of Caesar; they make the citizens leave.

Scenelet 2: Get Brutus on Our Side. Act 1, scene 2.

- **Characters and Motivations:** Cassius, a senator who is envious of Caesar and wants him removed from power; Brutus, a senator who wants a republic,[2] not a monarchy;[3] the Roman people, who want Caesar to be king.

- **Obstacles:** For Cassius, Brutus's honesty, conscience, and caution; for Brutus, the Roman people's will; for the Roman people, Caesar's reluctance to be king.

- **Conflict:**

  1. Cassius *versus* Caesar and Brutus;

  2. Brutus *versus* himself;

  3. Caesar *versus* the people.

Consequences: Cassius tries to convince Brutus to go against Caesar, and Brutus says he'll think about it; within earshot, off stage, Caesar says no when he is offered the crown three times.

Scenelet 3: Off Stage: Heard/Said about Caesar. Act 1, scene 2.

- **Characters and Motivations:** Cassius, a senator envious of Caesar and who wants him gone; Brutus, a senator who wants a republic,[4] not a monarchy;[5] Casca, a tribune who wants worship of Caesar to end.

- **Obstacles:** For Cassius, Caesar and his rise to power; for Brutus, Caesar and his rise to power; for Casca, the Roman people who worship Caesar.

- **Conflict:**

1. Cassius	*versus*	Caesar;
2. Brutus	*versus*	Caesar;
3. Casca	*versus*	the people.

Consequences: Casca gossips about Caesar being offered the crown three times by the people (whom he sees as stupid, obnoxious, and smelly); Cassius tells Casca to meet him later and Brutus to think of what's best for Rome.

Scenelet 4: Stormy Weather. Act 1, scene 3.

- **Characters and Motivations:** Cassius, a senator who is envious of Caesar and wants him removed from power; Casca, a tribune who thinks Caesar has grown too powerful; Nature, which wants to wreak destruction.

continued on next page

- **Obstacles:** For Casca, Nature, which scares him; for Cassius, Casca—if he is loyal to Caesar; for Nature, nothing.
- **Conflict:**
  1. Casca   *versus*   Nature;
  2. Cassius   *versus*   Casca;
  3. Nature   *versus*   everything.

Consequences: Casca is panicked by horrible, unnatural signs in Nature; Cassius panics that he has confessed too much to Casca, who might turn him in; Nature does whatever it wants.

1. Versus: from the Latin, meaning "against"
2. Republic: A form of government in which citizens hold the power, exercised by representatives (such as senators) whom citizens choose directly or indirectly
3. Monarchy: A form of government in which a king or queen holds power
4. Republic: A form of government in which citizens hold the power, exercised by representatives (such as senators) whom citizens choose directly or indirectly
5. Monarchy: A form of government in which a king or queen holds power

---

Handout 1.22A CR, Passing Up Pompey and Celebrating Caesar

A close reader asks you to understand events in the play and analyze them.

Background: Murellus tries to keep the streets safe while the people in the street celebrate because Caesar won a war against Pompey. Pompey was a ruler the people loved.

TEXT	ANNOTATION /TRANSLATION

You blocks, you stones, you worse than senseless things![1]

O you hard hearts, you cruel men of Rome,

Knew you not[2] Pompey? Many a time and oft[3]

Have you climb'd up to walls and battlements,

To towers and windows, yea,[4] to chimney tops,

Your infants[5] in your arms, and there have sat

The livelong[6] day, with patient expectation,

To see great Pompey pass the streets of Rome

Be gone!

1. Senseless things: Things without any feeling, inhuman
2. Knew you not . . . ?: Did you not know . . . ?
3. Oft: Often
4. Yea: Yes
5. Infants: Babies
6. Livelong: Whole
7. Heartless: Unkind, without feelings
8. Cruel: Mean, uncaring
9. Caprice: Unpredictability, ability to change suddenly

Directions: Answer these questions in complete sentences.

1. **GENERALIZATION:** Murellus is a tribune who is loyal to Caesar and angry at the Roman people. Reread the passage out loud in a voice that is angry.

continued on next page

2. **CAUSE AND EFFECT:** In Lines 1–2, Murellus says that the Roman people are heartless[7] and cruel.[8] Why is he telling the Roman people this? What have they done?

_____

_____

3. **SPECIFIC to GENERAL:** Murellus tells the people, "Be gone!" This is his solution to the problem. How do these words show his loyalty to Caesar?

_____

_____

_____

4. **VOCABULARY PRACTICE:** Write a story using new vocabulary you have just learned. Use any of these vocabulary words to create a story about a big idea.

Big Ideas: **LOYALTY**   **INGRATITUDE**   **CAPRICE**[9]

_____

_____

_____

_____

_____

_____

_____

_____

_____

5. **CAUSE AND EFFECT:** If Rome is celebrating Caesar, but Murellus tells people to stop, what could happen next? Guess three possibilities.

Option #1: _____

Option #2: _____

Option #3: _____

6. **KEY IMAGES:** Find three items in the passage to illustrate. Draw a scene or draw five separate images. Explain in one sentence for each why you chose these three.

Handout 1.22B CR, Passing Up Pompey and Celebrating Caesar

A close reader asks you to understand events in the play and analyze them.

Background: Murellus is a tribune who tries to keep order as workmen celebrate in the streets because Caesar won a civil war against his co-ruler, Pompey.

<u>TEXT</u>   <u>ANNOTATION/TRANSLATION</u>

You blocks, you stones, you worse than senseless things![1]

O you hard hearts, you cruel men of Rome,

Knew you not Pompey? Many a time and oft[2]

Have you climb'd up to walls and battlements,

To towers and windows, yea, to chimney tops,

Your infants in your arms, and there have sat

The livelong[3] day, with patient expectation,

To see great Pompey pass the streets of Rome

. . . And do you now put on your best attire[4]?

And do you now cull[5] out a holiday?

And do you now strew flowers in his way,

That comes in triumph over Pompey's blood?

Be gone!

1. Senseless things: Things without any feeling, inhuman
2. Oft: Often
3. Livelong: Whole
4. Attire: Clothing
5. Cull: Make into, choose

Directions: Answer these questions in complete sentences.

1. **GENERALIZATION:** Murellus is a tribune who is stern, bold, and loyal. Reread the passage aloud in a voice that fits such a character.

continued on next page

2. **GENERAL TO SPECIFIC:** Find four key words or phrases in the passage that prove Murellus's personality is stern, bold, and/or loyal.

_____ _____ _____ _____
Key Word/Phrase #1   Key Word/Phrase #2   Key Word/Phrase #3   Key Word/Phrase #4

3. **GENERALIZATIONS:** Find two adjectives that Murellus uses to describe the Roman citizens. _____ _____

4. **EVIDENCE:** Copy a quotation that Murellus uses to prove his descriptions of the citizens. _____
_____

5. **CAUSE AND EFFECT:** If Rome is celebrating Caesar, but Murellus tells people to stop, what do you think could happen next in the story? Guess three possibilities.

Option #1: _____
Option #2: _____
Option #3: _____

6. **DIGGING DEEPER INTO LANGUAGE:** Murellus calls the citizens of Rome, "You blocks, you stones . . . " He uses a metaphor: comparing two unlike things to each other to show an interesting connection. It is an equation: CITIZENS = BLOCKS/STONES. Explore these metaphors by starting a word family.

   a. Find any key words from the passage in the same family as *blocks* or *stones*.

   b. Go to the thesaurus and find words related to *blocks* or *stones* that could describe the citizens.

7. **GENERALIZATION:** Write a topic sentence to describe the citizens that uses descriptive words (adjectives). These may be key words or words from a word family.

   The citizens of Rome are considered blocks and stones by Murellus because they are _____, _____, and _____

8. **(CHALLENGE) EVALUATION:** Is Murellus being fair in the way he describes the citizens? Make a judgment of "Yes," "No," or "Maybe," and give three examples from the passage (paraphrased or quoted) to support your argument.

   a. _____
   b. _____
   c. _____

Teaching Julius Caesar: *A Differentiated Approach* © 2010 Lyn Fairchild Hawks.

Handout 1.22C CR, Passing Up Pompey and Celebrating Caesar

A close reader asks you to understand events in the play and analyze them. **Background:** Murellus is a tribune who tries to keep order as workmen celebrate in the streets because Caesar won a civil war against his co-ruler, Pompey.

TEXT	ANNOTATION /TRANSLATION

You blocks, you stones, you worse than senseless things![1]

O you hard hearts, you cruel men of Rome,

Knew you not Pompey? Many a time and oft[2]

Have you climb'd up to walls and battlements,

To towers and windows, yea, to chimney tops,

Your infants in your arms, and there have sat

The livelong[3] day, with patient expectation,

To see great Pompey pass the streets of Rome

. . . And do you now put on your best attire[4]?

And do you now cull[5] out a holiday?

And do you now strew flowers in his way,

That comes in triumph over Pompey's blood?

Be gone!

Run to your houses, fall upon your knees,

Pray to the gods to intermit[6] the plague

That needs must[7] light on this ingratitude.

1. Senseless things: Things without any feeling, inhuman
2. Oft: Often
3. Livelong: Whole
4. Attire: Clothing

continued on next page

5. Cull: Make into, choose

6. Intermit: Delay

7. Must: Should

Directions: Answer these questions in complete sentences.

1. **GENERAL TO SPECIFIC:** Murellus says to the Roman people: "O you hard hearts, you cruel men of Rome." Find two examples that Murellus feels justifies his accusation.

   Example #1:_____

   Example #2:_____

2. **GENERALIZATION:** What do you know about Murellus's personality from his actions and speech? Pick four key words or phrases to defend your interpretation of Murellus.

   _____ _____ _____ _____
   Key Word/Phrase #1   Key Word/Phrase #2   Key Word/Phrase #3   Key Word/Phrase #4

3. **CAUSE AND EFFECT:** If Murellus and Flavius feel so strongly Caesar should not be celebrated, what do you predict will happen to Murellus, Flavius, and Caesar? Guess three possible outcomes.

   Option #1: _____

   Option #2: _____

   Option #3: _____

4. **DIGGING DEEPER INTO LANGUAGE:** Murellus uses two metaphors to describe the citizens of Rome. Find them and explain: (a) any key words from the passage or thesaurus that further explain Murellus's choice of metaphor, or (b) challenge: how this metaphor might express a big idea of the play.

   _____ _____ _____ _____
   Key Word/Phrase #1   Key Word/Phrase #2   Key Word/Phrase #3   Key Word/Phrase #4

5. **GENERALIZATION:** Write a topic sentence to describe the first scene that uses key words from the passage. Hint: Your key words should be abstract nouns.

   The first scene of the play presents a situation in which characters are concerned about _____ and struggle with

   _____.

Handout 1.22D CR, Passing Up Pompey and Celebrating Caesar

Background: Murellus is a tribune who tries to keep order as workmen celebrate in the streets because Caesar won a civil war against his co-ruler, Pompey.

TEXT	ANNOTATION /TRANSLATION

You blocks, you stones, you worse than senseless things[1]!

O you hard hearts, you cruel men of Rome,

Knew you not Pompey? Many a time and oft[2]

Have you climb'd up to walls and battlements,

To towers and windows, yea, to chimney tops,

Your infants in your arms, and there have sat

The livelong[3] day, with patient expectation,

To see great Pompey pass the streets of Rome

. . . And do you now put on your best attire[4]?

And do you now cull[5] out a holiday?

And do you now strew flowers in his way,

That comes in triumph over Pompey's blood?

Be gone!

Run to your houses, fall upon your knees,

Pray to the gods to intermit[6] the plague

That needs must[7] light on this ingratitude.

1. Senseless things: Things without any feeling, inhuman
2. Oft: Often
3. Livelong: Whole
4. Attire: Clothing

continued on next page

5. Cull: Make into, choose

6. Intermit: Delay

7. Must: Should

Directions: Answer these questions in complete sentences.

1. **ANALYSIS:** Murellus's speech to the citizens is comprised of declarations and questions. What does he declare about the Romans? What does he question about them?

2. **EVALUATION:** Are you inclined to trust Murellus's assessment of the Romans as reliable or is his assessment unreliable? Why or why not? (Consider issues such as direct versus indirect characterization.)

3. **ANALYSIS:** Shakespeare introduces the play with a conflict between the tribunes and the common people over Caesar and whether to honor him. Identify three big ideas at work in this scene, and convert them to essential questions.

4. **ANALYSIS:** Caesar's character is in the background at this point, whereas Pompey's name is mentioned several times. Why? If the play is called *Julius Caesar*, why not begin the play with the protagonist? What questions or issues does Shakespeare's choice raise?

5. **DIGGING DEEPER INTO LANGUAGE:** Murellus uses blank verse, the language of nobility and monarchs, while the cobbler and carpenter speak in colloquial language. Each type of language has its own rhythm.

   a. Read aloud statements said by the men of both classes (tradesmen and tribunes).

   b. Scan five to ten lines of the cobbler and Murellus to find where the stresses fall.

   c. Make a list of key words that receive stresses.

   d. From this analysis, write a brief paragraph analyzing each character, stating what each man believes and values. Use key words and the emphasis provided by iambic pentameter to prove their beliefs and values.

      i. Make sure each paragraph has a topic sentence.

      ii. Make sure each paragraph has at least three examples.

Lessons 6–7: Hearkening Back to History

Phase 1, Analysis (90 minutes)

Begin with a WCA historical mini-lesson and then move to MR groups for historical role-play. Role-play in a WCA and end with WCA discussion.

This lesson offers an opportunity for students to simulate the political conflicts of Caesar's era, make predictions about events in the play, and practice the art of persuasion. Note that AS is a designation for many EUs, based on Jerome Bruner's proposition that any concept can be taught to any age in any intellectually honest fashion. You can explain verbal irony to a third grader—the firehouse burning down. Therefore, we must directly confront the misunderstanding that ELL and NOV students can't comprehend EUs.

Students will know:

- the definition of *exposition*: The beginning of the play where protagonists, conflict, setting, and big ideas are introduced (AS)
- the definition of *politics*: "(a) the art or science of government; (b) the art or science concerned with guiding or influencing governmental policy; (c) the art or science concerned with winning and holding control over a government." (Merriam-Webster)
- important historical events and context preceding Julius Caesar's rule (AS)

Students will be able to:

- make predictions about plot events based on the exposition (AS)

Students will understand:

- Julius Caesar's Rome was chaotic with rapid changes in leadership and loyalty (AS)
- Elizabethan England was likewise threatened with civil strife and issues of succession (AS)
- the first scene of a Shakespeare play sets the tone for the whole work (AS)
- in order for political factions to reconcile, all perspectives must be heard (AS)

- in order for political factions to prevail, persuasive strategies must be used (AS)
- reaching consensus is a challenging process requiring compromise and patience (AS)

Students will explore this question:

- What historical events must be understood to comprehend *Julius Caesar?* (AS)
- What strategies are most persuasive in writing and speaking? (AS)

Materials and Handouts

Use the following handouts and materials during this lesson. Most appear at the end of the lesson (page 79) unless otherwise noted to be at the companion website.

- Handouts 1.22, CR A–D; Handout 1.23, Historical Mini-Lesson: Rome in Caesar's Day; Handout 1.24, Student Notes: Rome in Caesar's Day; Handout 1.25, Group Profiles, A–D; and Handout 1.26, Problem-Solving at the All-School Meeting.
- A copy of Murellus's speech on the board or an overhead.
- A definition of exposition and politics on the board.
- An image of Rome in 44 B.C. Consider showing students this image: (http://upload.wikimedia.org/wikipedia/commons/7/76/RomanEmpire_Phases.png)
- Dictionaries and glossaries, one per student

Shakespeare's time harbored great contradictions. Medieval religious paradigms clashed with Renaissance thinking. Shakespeare rides this cusp of ambiguity, exploring the medieval framework of God in heaven and hell as punishment for evil, vis-à-vis the Renaissance questioning of these time-honored truths: Is God really watching, since evil people seem to get away with things? Are the rich and royal truly protected by divinity if they can lose their land and crowns? (Dye n. pag.) For more information on the zeitgeist of Shakespeare's era regarding civil strife and order, visit Michael Best's article "Crime" at the Internet Shakespeare Editions.

STEP 1. WCA: Recitation Regulars and Review of Homework (10 minutes)

1. Invite a student to perform in recitation regulars. Guide the class in effective feedback.

2. Review homework (Handouts 1.22, CR A–D). Ask students to read the definition of exposition, then at least ten or more lines from Murellus's speech.

   a. Characters: What do the speech and actions of Flavius and Murellus tell us about them? What are their motivations? (AS) What do we learn about Caesar from the opening scene, even though he is not present? (OT)

   b. Plot: What is the conflict and its obstacles? What do you predict will happen in the next scenes of the play? Why? (AS)

   c. Use other higher-level questions from CRs to involve students of all readiness levels in analyzing the exposition.

STEP 2. WCA: Historical Mini-Lesson (20 minutes)

1. Use Handout 1.23, Historical Mini-Lesson: Rome in Caesar's Day, to help students understand Roman history, Julius Caesar's biography, and Elizabethan political contexts. Distribute Handout 1.24, Student Notes: Rome in Caesar's Day and guide students in note-taking. Note that the act 1 quiz assesses knowledge from this lesson.

2. Show one or more film versions of the first scene of *Julius Caesar*. Ask students to identify aspects of Roman culture (festivals, transportation, government, and clothing or lack thereof) that compare or contrast with American culture. Students can compare this festival of Lupercal to an American inauguration of a new president or religious holiday.

3. Consider using Google Earth's Ancient Rome 3-D tour at http://earth.google.com/rome so that students can walk through the streets of Rome, circa 320 A.D.

The next activity is a problem-based learning activity in which you and students must tolerate a certain amount of ambiguity while they wrestle with the issue. The goal is for students to experience the complexity of issues facing a body politic and the diverse perspectives of its members. School issues needing solutions often include dress code, health and quality of cafeteria food, and homework load. Select an issue that engages your students in which they wish they had more voice. Establish the issue as a controversial proposition, such as, "The school dress code should require uniforms"; "Only foods low in transfat, sugar, and salt should be served in the cafeteria"; or "Each course should assign 30 minutes of homework per night."

STEP 3. MR Groups: Role-Play Preparation (20 minutes)

1. Explain to students they will now role-play the political situation of ancient Rome by applying its features to a modern context, school politics.

2. Review the definition of politics. Present the issue and the proposition. Announce that each will join one of four political factions to prepare for an all-school meeting to negotiate for power in a bloodless way—duking it out with words rather than daggers!

3. Divide the class into four groups and distribute Handouts 1.25, A–D, Group Profiles, and 1.26, Problem-Solving at the All-School Meeting.

> You should assign students to MR groups to ensure heterogeneity and that each includes students with strong speaking, leadership, and interpersonal skills.

   a. Group A will represent the faculty (senators); Group B, student government (tribunes); Group C, the student body (the people of Rome); and Group D, administration (the generals). To create accurate parallels to population numbers, make the largest group Group C and the smallest, D.

   b. Ask students to elect spokespersons and leaders for their groups, to prepare speeches, and to make decisions about the future of the school.

   c. Tell students that tomorrow at the all-school meeting each should prepare to "speak his piece" using ideas and evidence generated today.

   d. A spokesperson from each group will speak for two minutes to represent the group, and after that the floor will open for anyone else to speak for one minute each.

Homework Options

1. Ask students to prepare notes for their speech: a clear statement of the argument, at least three reasons, and supporting evidence for each reason.

2. *Independent Reading:* Ask students to read and annotate lines 1–24 (through the end of the scene between Caesar and the soothsayer) of scene 2, act 1. If you haven't introduced Mor-

timer Adler's coding system for annotation, you may want to do so now. Encourage students to make lists of key words and their connotations and to identify at least two big ideas at work in this scene.

Notes on Differentiation

1. *Roman History:* If you want to provide more historical context, ask an ADV student or a compacting student to provide a brief presentation on social class and roles in ancient Rome. The student can begin with Wikipedia (http://en.wikipedia.org/wiki/Social_class_in_ancient_Rome) and research other terms, such as *tribune*, on other sites (see http://www.livius.org/to-ts/tribune/tribune.html). This student can demonstrate how social roles such as tribunes evolved through different eras.

2. *Problem-Solving Activity:* Note the activity asks students to understand the roles (characters of) four groups at the school and to construct a persuasive argument. Use these assignments as informal pretests to discover who is astute at character analysis (six aspects of character), problem-solving, persuasion, role-play, group work, and performance. Keep these successes in mind as you find hooks to help students of all readiness levels succeed later on in essays and other standardized assessments.

3. *Homework:* Collect homework Handouts 1.22, CRs A–D, and see how well students are translating. Note the homework reading routine is now more open-ended, reinforcing annotation skills you have taught in class. This alternation between CRs and open-ended independent reading allows students some flexibility and also reduces your grading.

Phase 2, Performance

The following section of the lesson can take place on a separate day or as the second half of block period.

Materials Needed

Use the following handouts and materials during this lesson. Most appear at the end of the lesson (page 81) unless otherwise noted to be at the companion website.

- Proposition and rubric viewable to all students
- Podium
- Handouts 1.25, A–D, Group Profiles, and 1.26, Problem-Solving at the All-School Meeting

STEP 1. WCA and MR Groups: Role-Play Preparation (20 minutes)

1. Explain that this all-school meeting is an opportunity for each faction to convince the rest of the school to follow its lead. Review the four roles.

2. Present the challenges: How will each faction persuade the rest of the school? How will the body politic reach consensus?

3. Ask students to practice their speeches in groups for a few minutes.

STEP 2. WCA: Role-Play (30 to 90 minutes)

1. Seat students in a square formation where group members sit together and everyone can see each other. Place a podium at the front of the room.

2. Welcome everyone, stating you will be a mediator called in to reconcile the factions.

   a. Explain the goal is to explore the issue and work toward a resolution.

   b. State the ground rules: (a) state your argument clearly; (b) disagree respectfully; (c) keep to your time; and (d) encourage all group members to speak.

   c. Explain that each group's performance will be rated on the following rubric: (a) clarity of argument; (b) substance and persuasiveness of evidence; (c) participation and team-work; (d) respectful discussion; and (e) bonus—rhetorical style and poise.

   d. State the proposition to be debated. Draw from a hat the first group to speak.

3. Allow a spokesperson from each group to make a two-minute speech. After all speeches, call on members of each group to engage in discussion. Acknowledge successful speaking and debate behaviors, referencing the rubric as you compliment and guide.

4. With five minutes left, determine whether you will extend the debate longer over more periods or conclude it.

STEP 3. WCA: Reflection (10 minutes)
Lead students in reflecting about many perspectives to try to solve a complex issue.

1. What arguments were most convincing? Why? (AS)

2. Which group's arguments were clearest? Which group presented the most substantive evidence? (OT/ADV)

3. Which group appeared to be most unified? (AS)

4. Which group had the most rhetorical technique and the most poise? (OT/ADV)

5. Did one group seem more powerful than the other? Why? (AS)

6. How far apart are the various groups from reaching resolution at this time? (OT/ADV)

7. Which groups or individuals made the most significant efforts to reach resolution? (AS)

8. What would be required for the groups to reach consensus? (OT, ADV)

9. What did this experience teach you about the following:

    a. Characterization (AS)

    b. Conflict and obstacles (OT/ADV)

    c. Argument and persuasion (OT/ADV)

    d. Role-play and group work (AS)

    e. Politics (OT/ADV)

    f. Reaching consensus (OT/ADV)?

10. Draw equivalences on the board between ancient Roman politics and school politics: teachers = senators; student government = tribunes; student body = Roman citizens; and administration = generals or triumvirs. How might this simulation show similarities and differences between school politics and Roman politics in 44 B.C.? (ADV)

Homework Options

1. *Preassessment:* Ask students to write a speech—a persuasive paragraph—asking the school to take a certain action on the proposition, using any reasons or examples stated in class. Require 250 to 500 words, depending on your students' readiness levels.

2. *Independent Reading:* Ask students to read and annotate part of scene 2 between Cassius and Brutus, from "Will you go see the order of the course?" to "To all the rout, then hold me dangerous." Ask them to make a list of key words, their connotations, and big ideas.

Notes on Differentiation

1. *TQs:* How you tier questions for class discussion depends on your students' readiness levels; labels given here are only suggestions. Reflect on how your students respond to class discussion at this point in the unit:

    a. Which students are engaging fully, and which are still reticent? What do you think it might take to involve certain students in the exchange? How might you steer dominant speakers to listen better?

b. Which students do well at providing specific evidence for opinions? Which students do well at stating insightful generalizations? How can you recognize these successes? How can you encourage each type of speaker to hone different skills?

2. *Assessment of Persuasive Paragraphs.* This assignment pretests for one of the final writing assignments of this unit. Sort each student paragraph into one of four (or eight) groups to determine TR groups in writing instruction. Note in the following persuasive paragraph rubric that the ELL tiers assume the student struggles with vocabulary and syntax errors. Note also that students may overlap across tiers (an ELL student may be Tier 1 in organization, voice, and rhetorical style but Tier 2 in evidence and reasoning). Select from this table the knowledge and skills your students most need to learn and reduce the list of criteria. You can then scaffold to a longer list for the next unit.

Handout 1.23, Historical Mini-Lesson: Rome in Caesar's Day

Explain: Let's imagine today's date is 1599 and we're sitting in a class-room in Elizabethan England. This place is now called a *grammar school*. Look around: the only students here should be boys, ages seven and up, whose fathers can afford the fees. No girls allowed. Ladies, consider yourselves lucky if you *ever* learn to read and write: your main goal in life is to master cooking, cleaning, and sewing, or management of the household and servants if you're rich.

So what do you boys study all day? The language of Latin, its grammar, the writings of ancient Roman authors, and Roman history. Why not English? Latin is the international language for learning, not English! *English is a rough, growing language*; it's adopting new words from Latin every day. Recent poets and playwrights like Shakespeare are making English the language of literature. So you must learn how to write in Roman and Latin style, also known as the art of rhetoric (Gill 122).

What I'm about to share with you about ancient Rome, every kid in Elizabethan grammar school and Elizabethan theatergoers who came to see Shakespeare's *Julius Caesar* already know.

Direct: What four things did Elizabethan schoolboys study in grammar school? Write them in your student notes.

Explain: Shakespeare wrote *Julius Caesar* in 1599. Let's build a timeline of important dates.

Direct: In your notes, write "Shakespeare writes Julius Caesar" above 1599 A.D.

Explain: Before we place any more dates on the timeline, let's clarify "B.C." and "A.D." Can anyone define these acronyms? *Before Christ* and *Anno Domini* (Medieval Latin for "In the Year of Our Lord"). Christian churches in Western Europe used these to refer to two epochs—the time before Jesus and the time after. So let's record key B.C. and A.D. events:

1. Jesus of Nazareth was born in A.D. 1.
2. Julius Caesar was born in 100 B.C.
3. Julius Caesar was murdered in 44 B.C.
4. 1558 years later, Queen Elizabeth I was crowned—1558 A.D.
5. 1564 years later, William Shakespeare was born and, at the age of 35, he wrote this play.

What the boys of Elizabethan grammar schools knew was that Julius Caesar was a gifted leader, perhaps even a genius, and that ancient Rome in 44 B.C. was going through some political earthquakes. In what is today's Western Europe, Rome was *the* empire. Rome controlled the Western world and

continued on next page

parts of Asia. It was an expanding empire, thanks to generals like Pompey, Crassus, and Caesar.

Direct: Let's look at a map of the Roman Empire in 44 B.C. Where today is Italy? France? Spain? Germany?

Explain: By Caesar's death, the Roman Empire had conquered an impressive amount of what would become Europe. If you could lead so many different peoples and lands, you'd be an extremely powerful person. So who ran Rome? Three official groups:

- The senators and praetors: Legislators and judges like Cassius and Brutus who represented the patricians;

- The tribunes: Flavius and Murellus, elected by the plebeians, or working class of Rome, to represent and protect the people (Perry 7), but in the play you will see the tribunes act more like police officers; and

- The triumvirs: Generals like Caesar, Pompey, and Crassus who conquered new lands and kept the empire together with armies abroad.

- There were the people, or plebeians of Rome, but in Julius Caesar's day, they were not actively involved with the government as they had been in past eras.

Direct: Fill in your student notes to show this tenuous balance of power among the three groups. Beneath these three groups, write "the Roman people."

Explain: Caesar, Crassus, and Pompey were three generals who formed the first triumvirate—a balance of power among three men. The triumvirs joined to prevent Rome from entering into a civil war. Then Crassus is killed in battle; and later, Pompey and Caesar fight each other for power, and Caesar wins. Caesar becomes dictator for life. He starts a mission of reform, such as taking away the lands of patricians; lessening the power of the senate so it became more of an advisory council rather than a legislative body; and putting his picture on Roman currency (Gill N.S.). Several senators did not want Caesar as dictator, so they plotted against him, and killed him on the senate floor in 44 B.C.

In 1599, Queen Elizabeth was 66 years old. She had been queen for 45 years, which was longer than many Elizabethans even lived at that time. She was unmarried and had no children. Who would succeed her? What would happen? These were questions on the minds of Elizabethans who saw Shakespeare's play in 1599.

Direct: Write a list of thoughts in the minds of Elizabethans watching a play about *Julius Caesar*. Let's discuss: What parts of the world today have similar political troubles where succession and government organization is in doubt? Where have there been assassinations recently?

Handout 1.24, Student Notes: Rome in Caesar's Day

Name _____ Period _____ Date_____

What Elizabethan Boys in 1599 studied in grammar school:

I. _____

II. _____

III. _____

IV. _____

Why no one is studying English literature: _____
_____

Historical timeline:

100 B.C.   44 B.C.   A.D. 1   A.D. 1558   A.D. 1564   A.D. 1599

B.C. means _____ **A.D. means** _____

Rome in 44 B.C.

Kept together by generals, or triumvirs: _____, _____,
and _____

Meanwhile, back at home:

_____ and

The
Ancient
Roman
Empire

_____ fought over power.

Represented the _____ **Represented the** _____

Beneath these groups were the _____.

continued on next page

Caesar as Rex: Reforms

_____   _____   _____

What Elizabethans were thinking at the 1599 showing of *Julius Caesar*:

1. _____

2. _____

3. _____

Modern parallels:

Handout 1.25, A–D: Group Profiles for the All-School Meeting

Group A: You represent the faculty (like the senators of ancient Rome).

1. What jobs and responsibilities do teachers have?

2. Senators in ancient Rome wanted power over government legislation and budget. Make a parallel with teachers in a school: what rules and budget items might teachers want to influence?

3. What decisions can teachers make that affect the whole school?

4. How would faculty behave in an all-school meeting? How would physical demeanor appear? Speech? Actions?

Group B: You represent the student government (like the tribunes of ancient Rome).

1. What jobs and responsibilities does the student government have?

2. Ancient Roman tribunes (as portrayed in *Julius Caesar*) wanted power over the people and order in the streets. Make a parallel with student government— what power over other students and order might the student government want?

3. What decisions can the student government make that affect the whole school?

4. How would student government members behave in an all-school meeting? How would physical demeanor appear? Speech? Actions?

Group C: You represent the student body (like the citizens of ancient Rome).

1. What jobs and responsibilities do students have?

2. Citizens in ancient Rome wanted wealth and control over their own lives. Make a parallel with students in a school: what do students want to influence?

3. What decisions can students make that affect the whole school?

4. How would students behave in an all-school meeting? How would physical demeanor appear? Speech? Actions?

Group D: You represent the principal and assistant principals (like the triumvirs of ancient Rome).

1. What jobs and responsibilities do administrators have?

2. Triumvirs in ancient Rome wanted power over government legislation, budget, and military. Make a parallel with administrators in a school: what do administrators want to influence?

3. What decisions can administrators make that affect the whole school?

4. How would the principal and assistant principals behave in an all-school meeting? How would physical demeanor appear? Speech? Actions?

Handout 1.26, Problem-Solving at the All-School Meeting

Objective: To convince your classmates of your group's solution for a school issue.

The proposition: _____

Elect a group leader who will lead the group discussion and who will make sure everyone has a chance to speak at the meeting: _____
_____

Our group *AGREES DISAGREES* **(circle one) with the above proposition.**

Brainstorm a list of your group's main concerns. These should be issues related to the group's position in the school, the group's needs and wants, and the group's problems.

1. _____
2. _____
3. _____

List three arguments, the reasoning, and the evidence for each.

ARGUMENT   REASONING

1. _____   _____
   _____   _____
   _____   _____
   _____   _____

EVIDENCE (facts, statistics, sources, personal experiences, quotations, etc.)

_____
_____
_____
_____
_____

2. _____   _____
   _____   _____
   _____   _____

EVIDENCE: _____

_____
_____
_____
_____
_____

continued on next page

3. _____   _____
   _____   _____
   _____   _____
   _____   _____

EVIDENCE: _____
_____
_____
_____
_____
_____

Teaching Julius Caesar: *A Differentiated Approach* © 2010 Lyn Fairchild Hawks.

Handout 1.27, Persuasion Rubric

CRITERIA/READINESS LEVEL	ELL, Tier 1	ELL, Tier 2	NOV, Tier 1	NOV, Tier 2
Evidence & Reasoning	Demonstrates one of the following: -- claims are implied but not named in topic sentence -- attempt at evidence -- commentary may repeat evidence but not explain with reasoning or warrants	Demonstrates two of the following: -- claims are stated clearly at some point, if not in topic sentence -- one or more effective pieces of evidence -- commentary explains some evidence but not always with clear reasoning or warrants	Demonstrates one of the following: -- claims are implied but not named in topic sentence -- attempt at evidence -- commentary may repeat evidence but not explain with reasoning or warrants	Demonstrates two of the following: -- claims are stated clearly at some point, if not in topic sentence -- one or more effective pieces of evidence -- commentary explains some evidence but not always with clear reasoning or warrants
Organization, Voice, and Rhetorical Style	Demonstrates one of the following: -- attempt at topic sentence -- evidence or reasoning but not both	Demonstrates two or more of the following: -- clear or summative topic sentence -- evidence followed by commentary -- attempt at a persuasive tone or rhetorical flourish	Demonstrates two of the following: -- attempt at topic sentence -- evidence or reasoning but not both -- limited vocabulary with occasional use of new words	Demonstrates two or more of the following: -- clear or summative topic sentence -- evidence followed by commentary -- attempt at a persuasive tone or rhetorical flourish -- attempt at more expanded vocabulary and sophisticated sytax

CRITERIA/READINESS LEVEL	OT, Tier 1	OT, Tier 2	ADV, Tier 1	ADV, Tier 2
Evidence & Reasoning	Demonstrates two of the following: -- topic sentence summarizes some claims -- some effective supporting evidence with efforts to quote and paraphrase -- commentary explains most evidence with reasoning or warrants	Demonstrates two of the following: -- topic sentence argues all claims -- mostly effective supporting evidence, quoted and paraphrased, to include some data, statistics, definitions, analogies, causal analysis, first or secondhand sources, personal experience, quotations, or images -- commentary explains most evidence with clear reasoning or warrants	Demonstrates two of the following: -- topic sentence argues claims powerfully -- effective supporting details, quoted and paraphrased with some cited properly, to include at least two of the following: data, statistics, definitions, analogies, causal analysis, first or secondhand sources, personal experience, quotations, and/or images -- commentary defends all evidence with clear reasoning and warrants	Demonstrates all three: -- topic sentence argues all claims powerfully -- rich supporting evidence, balanced with paraphrase and quotation, all cited properly, to include two or more of the following: data, statistics, definitions, analogies, causal analysis, first or secondhand sources, personal experience, quotations, and/or images -- commentary defends all evidence with clear reasoning and warrants
Organization, Voice, and Rhetorical Style	Demonstrates two of the following: -- clear and summative topic sentence -- evidence followed by commentary, occasionally prefaced by context -- persuasive tone with some rhetorical flourish	Demonstrates two or more of the following: -- clear and summative topic sentence -- evidence followed by commentary, prefaced by context -- persuasive tone using one or more rhetorical devices such as anaphora, apostrophe, hypophora, figures of speech, or rhetorical questions	Demonstrates three or more of the following: -- clear and summative topic sentence -- commentary on evidence using effective transitions -- explanation of context for evidence -- persuasive tone using two or more rhetorical devices	Demonstrates three or more of the following: -- clear, summative, and precise topic sentence -- use of claim, reason, and warrant as commentary on evidence using effective transitions -- explanation of context for evidence -- effectively employs rhetorical devices -- strongly persuasive tone

Lesson 8: Building a Case

Writing Skills (120 minutes)

Begin with a WCA mini-lesson teaching writing skills, then move to MR or TR partners or groups for CR analysis. End with a WCA discussion and presentation.

This lesson offers an opportunity for students to analyze characters, make predictions about events in the play, and practice the art of persuasion.

At the end of the lesson, students will know:

- an element for compelling characterization is consuming emotion or need—a motivation (AS)
- the difference between round and flat characters (AS/OT)
- a satisfying sandwich paragraph contains a topic sentence and at least three significant details (AS)

Students will be able to:

- write a paragraph of argument using a topic sentence and three significant details (AS)
- write a paragraph of argument using a topic sentence, three significant details, context, and commentary (OT/ADV)

Students will understand:

- protagonists in a Shakespeare play are round characters (AS)
- convincing arguments require clear statements and compelling evidence (OT/ADV)

Students will explore this question:

- Who demonstrates character traits of loyalty, ambition, or envy at this stage of the play? (AS)

Materials and Handouts

Use the following handouts and materials during this lesson. Most appear at the end of the lesson (page 94) unless otherwise noted to be at the companion website.

- Handout 1.28, The Satisfying Sandwich Paragraph; and Handout 1.29, Building a Case for Loyalty, Ambition, or Envy.

- Visual of the satisfying sandwich paragraph posted.
- Big ideas posted: Loyalty, ambition, and envy.
- Brief outline
- Names of four protagonists posted—Caesar, Antony, Cassius, Brutus—on a board where students can write or tape up evidence around them.
- Index cards and markers
- Dictionaries and glossaries

Activities

STEP 1. WCA: Recitation Regulars, Mini-Quiz, and Mini-Lesson (30 minutes)

1. Invite a student to perform in recitation regulars. Guide the class in effective feedback.

2. (Optional): Give a mini-quiz. A mini-quiz is a ten-minute, open-book, and open-note quiz asking students to write about the prior night's reading on an index card: (a) two actions that characters took; (b) three key words and why they are key; (c) one big idea; (d) one quotation and its translation that proves the existence of the big idea; and (e) bonus: an explication of why this quotation proves the big idea.

> This mini-quiz is not only a snapshot of how well students read but also an informal pretest of student skill in offering context and commentary for evidence in literary analysis essays.

3. Explain to students that today they will play defense or prosecuting attorneys conducting research to determine the character of (a) future murderers (Cassius and Brutus), (b) a future victim of murder (Caesar), and (c) future avengers of murder (Antony).

4. Establish a real-world context to explain the role of character vis-à-vis criminal law:

    a. What makes criminal work hard is that sometimes crimes are complicated. It can be hard to say, *This person is 100 percent evil*, or, *This person is 100 percent good*. Why? People are complex, or *round*. One person may be guilty of a crime, but perhaps he or she acted in self-defense. Another person may act innocent, but perhaps he or she had malicious intent and was an accessory. Ask: who here has never made a mistake? Who here lacks any good qualities? No one. Who has never been envious? Ambitious? Loyal? Everyone is a mix of complex characteristics. So are Caesar, Antony, Cassius, and Brutus—the play's protagonists.

b. Good attorneys must determine cause and *motive* so justice can be served. Attorneys must examine the *character* of individuals. They must present *evidence* in compelling and organized formats. They must *persuade*.

5. Introduce the satisfying sandwich paragraph, a structure for effective writing, such as legal arguments. Teach the format using Handout 1.28 and use your character as material for a sample paragraph. Characterize yourself with a key trait in a topic sentence, defend it with three examples, and explain those examples using introductory context and elaborative commentary. Students' prior work on Handout 1.1, Character Diagram, will help build a self-descriptive paragraph.

STEP 2. TR Groups, CR Study (30 minutes)

1. Explain that if a murder will soon be committed in this play, students should examine the story for *cause* (as in, Caesar should have been removed from office because he's a tyrant and the murderers were protecting themselves and Rome) or *motive* (Cassius and Brutus had malicious intent toward Caesar). Three big ideas from the play—loyalty, ambition, and envy—will help in this research.

2. Provide a brief outline of the events of scene 2.

3. Assign students to TR groups (no more than four per group) to do a close reading of a section of scene 2 and do a character analysis using traits of loyalty, ambition, or envy.

   a. Using Handout 1.29, Building a Case for Loyalty, Ambition, or Envy, they must record all quotations from their section proving characters' loyalty, ambition, or envy. This is the skeleton of a satisfying sandwich paragraph.

   b. Assign Group 1 to ELL students; Group 2 to NOV; Group 3 to OT; and Group 4 to ADV.

   c. Circulate and provide guidance, reinforcing tips for tackling translation and helping students connect key words to big ideas. Remind students to keep in mind the six aspects of character, especially speech, action, thoughts, and what others say.

STEP 3. MR Groups, Jigsaw Decision (30 minutes)

1. Ask students to form groups of four to five where there is at least one representative from all four groups. Their purpose is to choose the most loyal, ambitious, or envious character. Who among the four stands out right now as most innocent (with loyalty) or most guilty (with ambition or envy)?

2. Groups should select a spokesperson who will share evidence that praises or condemns one of the four characters. Other group members should record quotations—key words or key phrases in quotation marks—on index cards to hold up as evidence during Step 4.

STEP 4. WCA Discussion (20 minutes)

1. Tell students to picture themselves as attorneys building a case, gathering the evidence. Show them the names posted—Caesar, Antony, Cassius, and Brutus. Who is most loyal, most ambitious, and most envious at this stage of the play?

2. Ask spokespersons from each group to come up to the names and pin quotations that prove a character's trait on the character.

3. Encourage students to disagree and produce counterevidence. Remind students that at this stage, there is not a final answer until the murder has occurred and the consequences of that murder have been played out with character choices.

Homework Options

1. Assign TR reading:

   a. Challenge Level 1 (ELL–NOV): Read and annotate lines 79–99 (from "What means this shouting?" to "Endure the winter cold as well as he") of scene 2, act 1. Make a list of key words and their connotations. Identify where you see envy.

   b. Challenge Level 2 (OT): Read and annotate lines 79–130 (from "What means this shouting?" to "And bear the palm alone") of scene 2, act 1. Make a list of key words and their connotations. Identify at least two big ideas besides envy.

   c. Challenge Level 3 (ADV): Read and annotate lines 79–177 (from "What means this shouting?" to ". . . show of fire from Brutus") of scene 2, act 1. Analyze Cassius's speech. Identify (a) his goal of persuasion and (b) his strategies for convincing Brutus. Evaluate strategies and determine which one is most effective.

> You can allow students to choose challenge levels, since at this stage you are still assessing comprehension and translation skills to determine TR groups. For tips on how to present varying levels of challenge, refer to Appendix B, Grading in a Differentiated Classroom, page 214. A discreet way to assign TR homework reading is to return mini-quiz cards with a number on the back —1, 2, or 3—to let students know your recommended reading plan for that night.

Notes on Differentiation

TR readings in the Handout 1.29 activity, Building a Case for Loyalty, Ambition, or Envy, are selected not only based on length but also complexity. Some parts of the scene may not directly mention loyalty, ambition, or envy, but actions and context prove these character traits exist. You may need to assist OT and ADV students to make that analytical leap.

Designing the Remainder of Act 1 Lessons

How will you lead students through the remainder of act 1?

Recommended Reading Schedule

- Decide which scenes are key to understanding act 1 and design CRs to help students thoroughly analyze these passages. Alternate with independent reading and annotation.
- With independent reading, ask students to read between 20 to 100 lines, using your recommended resources. Tasks should include direct translation, annotation, and analysis. Make sure that reading questions challenge all readiness levels.

Designing CRs

When reading closely, students should strive to comprehend and actively interpret rather than build a list of plot events.

CRs should provide a brief amount of text, space to translate and annotate, and critical thinking questions of several types. Here are suggested options for varying readiness levels.

Besides the CR, students can try the game of Tic-Tac-Toe (see page 96).

ELL/NOV reading questions: (Note that the analytical questions prepare students for paragraph writing—generalizations balanced with evidence—and focus on cause and effect.)

- GENERAL TO SPECIFIC: If a character has *x* trait, which quotations from the passage prove this trait exists?
- VOCABULARY PRACTICE: What synonyms can you find for this trait?
- CAUSE AND EFFECT: Why does this character take this action? What are/might be the consequences of these actions?
- KEY WORD SEARCH: Find abstract nouns in this passage. Find adjectives and verbs. Circle those that seem the most important. What big ideas do you see?

- DIGGING DEEPER INTO LANGUAGE: What connotations do you see in word choice in the figurative language?

OT/ADV reading questions:

- GENERAL TO SPECIFIC: This character says _____ about another character. Find at least one example justifying this indirect characterization.

- GENERALIZATION: What do you know about a character's personality from his actions and speech? Pick four key words or phrases to defend your interpretation.

- CAUSE AND EFFECT: If this character took that action, what do you predict will happen next? Guess three possible outcomes.

- EVALUATION: Is the character's point of view reliable or unreliable? Why or why not? (Consider issues such as direct versus indirect characterization.)

- ANALYSIS: What big ideas are at work in this scene? Convert them to essential questions.

- ANALYSIS: Why characterize/create conflict/establish setting in this manner? What other choices might the playwright have made instead?

- DIGGING DEEPER INTO LANGUAGE: How does figurative language affect character and setting description? How does iambic pentameter reinforce the big ideas of the passage?

Suggested Passage for CRs

- Cassius and Brutus, scene 2: "Tell me, good Brutus, can you see ... To all the rout, then hold me dangerous." (Big ideas: appearance, ambition, deception, honor, manipulation, persuasion)

- Cassius and Brutus, scene 2: "Why, man, he doth bestride. . . . show of fire from Brutus." (ambition, envy, deception, free will, glory, love, manipulation, patriotism, persuasion)

- Caesar and Antony, scene 2: "Let me have men about me that are fat ... and tell me truly what thou think'st of him." (appearance, ambition, courage, envy, fear, frailty, loyalty, trust)

- Casca's two monologues, scene 2: "I can as well be hanged ... receiving the bad air" and "Marry, before he fell down. . . . they would have done no less." (ambition, caprice, glory, honor, leadership, loyalty)

- Cassius's soliloquy, scene 2: "Well, Brutus, thou art noble ... or worse days endure." (ambition, conspiracy, honor, love, manipulation, persuasion, trust)

- Cassius, scene 3: "You are dull, Casca . . . as these strange eruptions are." (ambition, chaos, conspiracy, courage, fate, fear, nature, persuasion, power)
- Cassius's and Casca's dialogue, scene 3: "I know where I will wear this dagger then. . . . As who goes farthest." (conspiracy, courage, frailty, free will, loyalty)

Tic-Tac-Toe

Tic-Tac-Toe serves as a CR activity to review reading and encourage discussion. You can scaffold it for all levels of Bloom's Taxonomy: questions can focus on knowledge, comprehension, application, analysis, synthesis, and evaluation.

Knowledge questions: *Who, what, when, where?* Students identify character and plot facts.

Comprehension questions: *What, how, and in what way?* Students identify plot events, character emotions, and character choices.

Application questions: *What's next or what do you suggest?* Students apply their knowledge of plot and character to big ideas.

Analysis questions: *How, why, where do you see a pattern, and what if?* Students analyze process, cause and effect, patterns and trends, make predictions, and make comparisons and contrasts using metaphor, simile, and analogy.

Synthesis questions: *What is the theme and how would you summarize?* Students identify big ideas, essential questions, and essential understandings as they grasp character and plot as unified entities.

Evaluation questions: *Should, is it good, is it right, is it quality, is it appropriate?* Students make judgments based on criteria of quality, ethics, preference, and taste.

Use and Management: A = Novice, B = On-Target, and C = Advanced. Students can complete the game solo or in partners. This assignment can function as homework and classwork or as an alternate to a final quiz for each act. In partners, the game is harder, simply because the student must take questions from any row to win. Students can use their books or work from memory. Students can also develop questions for another advanced version of Tic-Tac-Toe.

Grading: You can award points when answers meet a certain criteria. Criteria can be any skill focus, such as substantive evidence to defend an answer, commentary on evidence, strong topic sentences, and so forth.

Handout 1.28, The Satisfying Sandwich Paragraph

TOPIC SENTENCE[1]: I am _____.

CONTEXT[2]: _____
_____

EVIDENCE: (detail #1)[3] _____
_____
_____

COMMENTARY[4]: _____
_____

CONTEXT: _____
_____

EVIDENCE: (detail #2) _____
_____

COMMENTARY: _____
_____

CONTEXT: _____
_____

EVIDENCE: (detail #3) _____
_____

COMMENTARY: _____
_____
_____

1. **TOPIC SENTENCE** is the bread, organizing the paragraph, keeping it together
2. **CONTEXT** is the vegetables, a healthy introduction that helps the tasty protein make sense or digest better
3. **EVIDENCE** is the protein, the substance that fills you up and convinces you you're full
4. **COMMENTARY** is the cheese, adding flavor and balance that compliments and extends the protein

Teaching Julius Caesar: *A Differentiated Approach* © 2010 Lyn Fairchild Hawks.

Handout 1.29, Building a Case for Loyalty, Ambition, or Envy

Directions:

1. Read your assigned section.

   a. Group 1: Caesar: "Forget not in your speed . . ." to Antony: "When Caesar says, 'Do this,' it is perform'd."

   b. Group 2: Cassius: "Why, man, he doth bestride . . ." to " . . . That he is grown so great?"

   c. Group 3: Caesar: "Let me have men . . ." to " . . . tell me truly what thou think'st of him."

   d. Group 4: Casca: "I can as well be hanged . . . very loath to lay his fingers off it" and Cassius: "Well, Brutus, thou are noble . . . or worse days endure."

2. Translate and annotate with the help of your group members.

   a. Do you find any key words synonymous[1] with *loyalty, ambition,* or *envy*? Any derivations[2] of these words? Any word families?

   b. What are connotations of the key words? Find at least four for each.

3. Complete one or more topic sentences with (a) an adjective (*loyal, ambitious,* or *envious* and (b) quoted evidence—key words, key phrases, including the verse number. You can break up one quotation into multiple pieces of evidence.

Caesar is _____ (adjective) because

Quotation #1: _____

Quotation #2: _____

Quotation #3: _____

Antony is _____ (adjective) because

Quotation #1: _____

Quotation #2: _____

Quotation #3: _____

Cassius is _____ (adjective) because

Quotation #1: _____

Quotation #2: _____

Quotation #3: _____

Brutus is _____ (adjective) because

Quotation #1: _____

Quotation #2: _____

Quotation #3: _____

1. Synonymous: Similar or equivalent in meaning; expressing the same idea

2. Derivations: Words originating from bases of other words, such as the word *ambitious* is a derivation of *ambition*

Teaching Julius Caesar: *A Differentiated Approach* © 2010 Lyn Fairchild Hawks.

Tic-Tac-Toe A

Directions:

1. Play the game of Tic-Tac-Toe to win. When you land on a square, answer the question.

2. Your answer must contain:

   a. A topic sentence,

   b. Two examples from the text, and

   c. An explanation of why you chose these examples.

Knowledge	Knowledge	Knowledge
Why are the Roman citizens celebrating in the streets when the play opens?	Why are Flavius and Murellus so angry at the Roman citizens? What is the tribunes' solution?	What do the Roman citizens insist Caesar do, but he refuses?
Comprehension	**Comprehension**	**Comprehension**
Why does Cassius pull Brutus aside for a conversation? What is the main point of what Cassius tells Brutus?	What is Brutus's decision regarding what Cassius says?	What is Casca's attitude about what happened with Caesar, Antony, and the citizens?
Application	**Application**	**Application**
Where do you see the big idea of *fear* in act 1? What consequences might this fear have later?	Where do you see the big idea of *envy* in act 1? What consequences might this envy have later?	Where do you see the big ideas of *loyalty* and *patriotism* in act 1? What consequences might these feelings have later?

Tic-Tac-Toe B

Directions:

1. Play the game of Tic-Tac-Toe to win. When you land on a square, answer the question.

2. Your answer must contain:

   a. A topic sentence,

   b. Two examples from the text, and

   c. An explanation of why you chose these examples.

Comprehension	Comprehension	Comprehension
Why does Cassius pull Brutus aside for a conversation? What is the main point of what Cassius tells Brutus?	What is Brutus's decision regarding what Cassius says?	What is Casca's attitude about what happened with Caesar, Antony, and the citizens?
Application	**Application**	**Application**
Where do you see the big idea of *fear* in act 1? What consequences might this fear have later?	Where do you see the big idea of *envy* in act 1? What consequences might this envy have later?	Where do you see the big ideas of *loyalty* and *patriotism* in act 1? What consequences might these feelings have later?
Analysis	**Analysis**	**Analysis**
What are the differences between Casca's, Cicero's, and Cassius's attitudes about the stormy weather and odd events in nature?	Cassius is like . . . ? Use a metaphor, simile, or analogy to describe him.	What do we know about Caesar as a leader so far? Why might these details be important later?

Tic-Tac-Toe C

Directions:

1. Play the game of Tic-Tac-Toe to win. When you land on a square, answer the question.

2. Your answer must contain:

   a. A topic sentence,

   b. Two examples from the text, and

   c. An explanation of why you chose these examples.

Application	Application	Application
Where do you see the big idea of *fear* in act 1? What consequences might this fear have later?	Where do you see the big idea of *envy* in act 1? What consequences might this envy have later?	Where do you see the big ideas of *loyalty* or *patriotism* in act 1? What consequences might these feelings have later?
Analysis	**Analysis**	**Analysis**
What are the differences between Casca's, Cicero's, and Cassius's attitudes about the stormy weather and odd events in nature?	Cassius is like . . . ? Use a metaphor, simile, or analogy to describe him	What do we know about Caesar as a leader so far? Why might these details be important later?
Evaluation	**Evaluation**	**Evaluation**
What is Brutus's concern about following Cassius's plan? What should Brutus do?	Is Caesar's assessment of Cassius correct?	Is Cassius's assessment of Caesar correct?

Big Ideas in Act 1: A Reference Guide for the Teacher

See quotations that evidence big ideas at work and search the text to find more.

The Big Idea of **AMBITION:** **act 1, scene 1,** **Flavius:** "These growing feathers pluck'd from Caesar's wing/ Will make him fly an ordinary pitch, Who else would soar above the view of men/ And keep us all in servile fearfulness."	*The Big Idea of* **APPEARANCE:** **act 1, scene 1,** **Flavius:** "What, know you not/ Being mechanical, you ought not walk/ Upon a labouring day without the sign/ Of your profession?"
The Big Idea of **CAPRICE:** **act 1, scene 1,** **Murellus:** "O you hard hearts, you cruel men of Rome/ Knew you not Pompey?"	*The Big Idea of* **CHAOS:** **act 1, scene 2,** **Casca:** ". . . the rabblement hooted, and clapped their chopped hands, and threw up their sweaty nightcaps, and uttered such a deal of stinking breath . . . "
The Big Idea of **CONSPIRACY:** **act 1, scene 2,** **Brutus:** "Into what dangers would you lead me, Cassius . . . ?"	*The Big Idea of* **CONSTANCY:** **act 1, scene 2,** **Cassius:** "Thy honourable metal may be wrought/ From at it is dispos'd. Therefore it is meet/ That noble minds keep ever with their likes;/ For who so firm that cannot be seduc'd?"
The Big Idea of **COURAGE:** **act 1, scene 2,** **Caesar:** "I rather tell thee what is to be fear'd/ Than what I fear: for always I am Caesar."	*The Big Idea of* **COWARDICE:** **act 1, scene 2,** **Cassius:** "'Tis true, this god did shake,/ His coward lips did from their colour fly . . ."

The Big Idea of ENVY:
act 1, scene 2,
Cassius:

"Why, man, he doth bestride the narrow world /
Like a Colossus, and we petty men /
Walk under his huge legs and peep about /
To find ourselves dishonourable graves."

The Big Idea of FEAR:
act 1, scene ___,
_____:

"_____
_____
_____."

The Big Idea of DECEPTION:
act 1, scene 2,
Cassius:
"I will this night, /
In several hands, in at his windows throw, /
As if they came from several citizens, /
Writings . . . "

The Big Idea of FREE WILL:
act 1, scene ___,
_____:

"_____
_____
_____."

The Big Idea of FATE:
act 1, scene ___,
_____:

"_____
_____
_____."

The Big Idea of GLORY:
act 1, scene ___,
_____:

"_____
_____
_____."

The Big Idea of FRAILTY:
act 1, scene ___,
_____:

"_____
_____
_____."

More Big Ideas to Research

HEROISM	HONESTY	HONOR	IDEALISM
INGRATITUDE	LEADERSHIP	LOVE	LOYALTY
MANHOOD	MANIPULATION	NATURE	PATRIOTISM
PERSUASION	POWER	REALISM	REVENGE
TRUST			

Act 2

Introduction

The Philosophy behind Act 2

By now your students are familiar with the whole-part-whole flow of class and reading routines that alternate between CR analysis and independent annotation. This is an excellent time to assess their progress. How well are your students probing the text? How well are they performing it? Are they able to keep the big ideas in focus? How well do they respond to MR and TR activities?

During act 2, you can adjust goals in response to student performance. Continue to diagnose readiness, identify interests, and address learning styles. You can reinforce translation skills and intensify the search for key words and big ideas. You can continue to make analysis, community, and celebration a priority.

What's in Store

In this chapter you will find:

- A sample lesson;
- An Internet investigation;
- A sample CR followed by a list of suggested CR passages;
- Writing instruction and motif mini-lessons;
- Design tips for developing a performance lesson; and
- A suggested act 2 quiz.

See what parts of *Julius Caesar* spark the most enthusiasm. What new lessons could you create that might be driven by student interests?

Companion Website

The scholar's seat: Respond to critics' interpretations about Brutus's character and tragic heroes.

To access the companion website, visit http://www.lynhawks.com, click on Shakespeare's image, and log in with username (bard) and password (caesar). Go to the act 2 section.

Suggested Calendar

This calendar is a sample guide for pacing lessons throughout the unit.

MONDAY	TUESDAY	WEDNESDAY	THURSDAY	FRIDAY
When in Rome Homework: CR 2.4 A–D, Brooding Brutus	*When in Rome* Homework: TR independent reading	*When in Rome* Homework: Creative writing	Mini-Lesson: *Pin the Tail on the Donkey* Homework: CR	Mini-Lesson: *Pin the Tail on the Donkey* Homework: TR independent reading
Mini-Lesson: *Let's Make a Motif Motto* Homework: CR	Cue cards or motive matchsticks Homework: TR independent reading	Perform excerpts of scene 2. Film clip. Homework: CR or independent reading	Perform excerpts of scenes 3–4. Film clip. Homework: Study for quiz	Act 2 Quiz

Lesson 1: When in Rome

Internet Investigation (140 minutes)

Begin with a WCA (mini-lesson on research skills), then move to TR partners for Internet research. Move to MR groups for jigsaw sharing, followed by WCA discussion.

> This lesson helps students learn note-taking and paraphrasing skills while learning about the play's historical context.

Students will know:

- Roman ideals for character (AS)
- Roman political and governmental values (AS)
- Julius Caesar's tremendous accomplishments (AS)
- the definitions of paraphrase, summary, and academic honesty (AS)
- the definition of EQs (AS)

Students will be able to:

- search websites to identify key facts that answer a search question (AS)
- paraphrase key facts and quotations into academically honest language (OT/ADV)
- cite sources properly (AS)
- summarize key facts and quotations into academically honest language (OT/ADV)
- pose EQs (AS)

Students will understand:

- we must use the text to determine big ideas and EUs (AS)
- ancient Romans valued honor, bravery, Stoicism, Epicureanism, and ambition (AS)
- Julius Caesar was an accomplished and heroic historical figure (AS)
- academic honesty means using your own words in your own order and giving credit where credit is due (OT/ADV)

Students will explore these questions:

- What did Romans value in government and character? (AS)
- How are the big ideas of *Julius Caesar* reflected in the history of ancient Rome? (OT/ADV)

Materials and Handouts

Use the following handouts and materials during this lesson. Most appear at the end of the lesson (page 109) unless otherwise noted to be at the companion website.

- Handout 2.1, Right Ways to Research; Handout 2.2, Internet Investigation: Reaching Back to Rome; Handout 2.3, Satisfying Sandwich of Key Facts; and Handouts 2.4 A–D, CR: Brooding Brutus
- Big ideas posted (as seen in Handout 1.7, Big Ideas Interest Inventory, or Handout 1.8, Digging Up Themes in *Julius Caesar*)
- Search questions posted: What did the ancient Romans value in their government? What did ancient Romans value in individuals? Why was Julius Caesar considered a hero?
- Internet access

Companion Website

All Web links are available at the companion site so you can copy and paste them onto your own Web page. To access the companion website, visit http://www.lynhawks.com, click on Shakespeare's image, and log in with username (bard) and password (caesar). Go to the act 2 section.

Activities

STEP 1. WCA: Introduction and Mini-Lesson (30 minutes)

1. Invite a student to perform a recitation. Lead students in providing effective feedback.
2. Explain to the students the importance of walking in the shoes of ancient Romans in order to better understand the big ideas of this play.
3. Introduce the concepts of the search question, key facts, and academic honesty using Handout 2.1, Right Ways to Research.

STEP 2. TR Pairs (50 minutes)

1. Introduce the activity of Internet research, or Web questing, using Handouts 2.2, Satisfying Sandwich of Key Facts and Handout 2.3, Internet Investigation: Reaching Back to Rome (see http://www.lynhawks.com), and ask students to choose the search question that interests them the most.
2. Place students in TR pairs (research prompt A is for ELL/NOV; B, for OT; and C, for ADV). Their task is to search the Web and outline satisfying sandwich paragraphs using Handout 2.2, Satisfying Sandwich of Key Facts, to share in jigsaw groups later. Note to students that the last act is to write a topic sentence—an answer to the search question that summarizes the key facts with abstract nouns and adjectives.

Depending on readiness levels, you may want to model some sample topic sentences, such as *The ancient Romans valued ___, ___, and ___;* or *The ancient Romans valued ___, ___, and ___;* or *Julius Caesar was considered a hero because of _____, _____, and _____* . Since you are teaching the thinking for essay writing—the movement from concrete details to abstract generalizations—some students will need a model of the topic sentence or thesis formula. Note three spaces for abstract nouns and adjectives. This is formulaic but not required. See the sample mini-lesson on page 129 for more information.

STEP 3. MR Groups, Jigsaw (30 minutes)

    1. Ask students to form groups of three to five students each so that students who answered all three prompts are represented in each group.

        a. First task: Read search questions and then present outlines to one another.

        b. Second task: Answer an essential question together: How are the big ideas of *Julius Caesar* reflected in ancient Rome's history?

STEP 4. WCA, Reporting Back (30 minutes)

Ask each group to report and refer to the posted big ideas as they explain historical detail in light of the ideas of the play.

Do you have access to a shared Web space where students can build a wiki or a blog? Have students post their satisfying sandwich paragraphs there and offer credit for students who use the satisfying sandwich rubric to critique one another's work as well. Call it the Roman Forum!

Homework Options

    1. Ask students to complete Handout 2.4 CR, Brooding Brutus, A–D.

    2. Offer a creative writing skill prompt:

        a. Prompt #1: We only get fragments of the scrolls tossed through Brutus's window: let's get the full story! Write the letter Brutus receives from an anonymous Roman. **Role:** Cassius, pretending to be an anonymous Roman citizen. **Audience:** Brutus. **Format:** Letter, which can use some of the language Brutus reads aloud in act 2, scene 1. **Themes:** Express what is being said about the big ideas of *patriotism*, *loyalty*, and *revenge*.

        b. Prompt #2: Write the oath that the conspirators might have said together if Brutus hadn't stopped them. Why are these men so dedicated to removing Caesar from power? **Role:** Conspirator. **Audience:** Each other, and the cause. **Format:** Oath. **Theme:** Express what is being said about the big ideas of *loyalty*, *honesty*, *patriotism*, and / or *envy* and *revenge*.

RAFT assignments are creative writing assignments with a formula of Role, Audience, Format, Theme. They are excellent ways to have students walk in the shoes of characters and explore the big ideas of the play. Choose among a variety of formats, such as letters, speeches, songs, poems, dialogues, short stories, memos, and so forth.

Notes on Differentiation

1. The mini-lesson, Right Ways to Research, uses the New Criticism approach—turning to the text as the main source of evidence. Another project for ADV students could be researching various schools of criticism and using those different lenses to view the play.

2. For the skill of paraphrasing, you may wish to provide a special mini-lesson to ensure that students know how to take meaningful notes without copying and to give credit where credit is due. The OWL at Purdue University is an excellent online resource, as is an online, independent study writing course for gifted students offered by the Duke University Talent Identification Program, *The Writer's Journey, Volume 2*. Keep in mind that mini-lessons might be best used in TR groups, when you need to provide special instruction to a group of one readiness level when certain students need remediation or acceleration.

3. The Internet investigation is an introduction to research skills, focusing mostly on questioning strategies that drive good research, and outlining skills necessary for writing a substantive paragraph. Note the differences between level A search questions and levels B and C: Level A is given mostly knowledge, or closed questions, with the option of a higher-level analysis question, as well as guiding questions to help students answer the closed question. Level A is for ELL and NOV students who need extra time with reading the Web pages and time to take paraphrased and cited notes. Paraphrasing requires analysis and vocabulary fluency, so it is ample work for ELL/NOV students.

   a. Since you are providing sources, students aren't required to vet sites for legitimacy, which is another skill worthy of a mini-lesson. You may want to give your students tips on how to distinguish between legitimate and illegitimate online sources, especially if they search beyond your recommendations.

   b. For ADV students needing further challenge, you might require that their satisfying sandwich answer outlines offer context introducing each example and commentary explaining how each example answers the question.

4. For Homework Handout 2.4 CR, Brooding Brutus, A–D:

    a. Note that version A models topic sentences illustrating big ideas. It also asks students to master new vocabulary and build sentences with parts of speech that express big ideas (*ambition* expressed as *ambitious,* or *deception* expressed as *deceived*). Building this fluency and a more expanded vocabulary is key to the process of abstraction when creating a topic sentence.

    b. Version B introduces the skill of commentary on examples and asks students to take the connotations they derive from metaphor to pinpoint Brutus's assessment of Caesar. Understanding that the smallest word or phrase can be resonant with associations and that it can be linked back to a topic idea (topical subgroups and key words) is essential to building a topic sentence.

    c. Version C asks students to rely on references and a stronger vocabulary in order to translate; it also asks them to independently draw conclusions (in the form of topic sentences) and prove them using examples and commentary. Understanding that one's conclusions should be defended with both examples and commentary is key to an on-target and higher-level literary analysis.

    d. Version D asks ADV students to analyze and evaluate character actions and prove their arguments using examples and commentary. Evaluation—analysis by criteria—requires a thorough defense with rich examples and commentary.

    e. CR assignments contain many questions. You may choose to use all questions and provide both class time and multiple homework opportunities to complete one CR, or, you may prefer to select certain questions you believe are key to comprehending and analyzing the scene. Note the high level of sophistication required in level D's CR, and remember that ADV students pursuing compacting should complete D-level CRs whenever possible.

Handout 2.1, Mini-Lesson: Right Ways to Research

Explain: Like all great literature, *Julius Caesar* is a play driven by big ideas.
Direct: Let's look at our list of big ideas that appear in the play. Turn to a partner and choose at least three big ideas that sound like values, which are beliefs people follow and use to direct their lives . Search for American-sounding values and ancient Roman values. (Suggested answers include *ambition, honor, loyalty, patriotism*, and so forth).

Explain: These are big ideas we will understand better by testing them against Shakespeare's play. Shakespeare was an author who, like any of us, had an opinion about these values. Since he's not here to tell us, "Hey, this is what I *really* meant," all we have is the text to analyze. So we need to ask some tough questions, the kind that keep you up at night, ones people still try to answer today. In science it might be, *How do we cure this disease?* In politics it might be, *How do we get two warring countries to make peace?* In literature, it might be, *Why do people do evil deeds? Is Caesar a real hero or a martyr? Brutus? Antony? Cassius?*

In this Internet investigation, your research will be driven by three essential questions, also known as search questions: *What did the ancient Romans value in their government? What did ancient Romans value in individuals? Why was Julius Caesar considered a hero?*

Essential questions investigate big ideas and search for answers to tough questions. Essential questions are not one-answer questions or yes/no questions. They can't be answered by only statistics and facts. They are questions that you will wrestle with for a while.

Direct: Turn to a partner and create a closed question about act 1 of *Julius Caesar*—a question with one factual answer only, that no one will argue. The answer could be a number, a color, a date, or a basic piece of information someone can easily find by reading the play.

Explain: Let's hear some examples. (Suggestions: What does Antony try to do in front of the crowd but Caesar refuses? Answer: Crown him.) Now, this answer is an important detail but also a dead end in terms of interesting investigation. It's not a good question to spend a whole day researching because you can answer it by turning to a page. But, that answer might help answer a question about Caesar's ambitions or Antony's loyalty. Let's take a moment to discuss what we call essential questions: *Does Caesar seem ambitious during this pretend-crowning ceremony? Does Antony seem loyal? Ambitious? In other words, how loyal or ambitious are these men overall?* These questions are open because people may have different opinions, just as lawyers might argue in a court of law over someone's innocence or guilt.

Direct: Let's hear some thoughts. Let's turn to Casca's report in scene 2 of the crowning, beginning at "Why, there was a crown offered him . . . " (Reread

continued on next page

the scene until "receiving the bad air." Repeat each question, get opinions, and encourage students to use the text to defend their positions.)

Explain: See how we have argument about this issue? See how we're tackling challenging subjects—analyzing people's characters and whether people have good, evil, or self-centered intentions? We are wondering how much we can trust these two men to do the right thing for Rome, and we need to keep watching for answers throughout the play. Arguing tells us we have good search questions. Note also the big ideas we use when we pose the questions—loyal for loyalty, ambitious for ambition. So, let's discuss how you will answer the search questions during an Internet investigation. Here's the process:

- Ask the search question. (Make sure it's open and essential and not closed.)
- Look for key facts to answer it. (Does the fact answer the question?)
- Paraphrase those key facts. (Are my notes my own words—no copying—and my own order?)
- Cite each fact. (What's the source? Have I given credit where credit is due?)

It might help you to remember to CLAP yourself on the back—which is checking to see that you have Cited correctly, Looked for key facts, Asked an open question, and Paraphrased well.

Why do we cite and paraphrase? Academic honesty. We give credit where credit is due. If you aren't the person who found the facts you're recording—in other words, the person who completed the archaeological dig, wrote the history text, studied the topic for years, went to college to learn how to write about history, or posted that history website, then chances are, you owe the original archaeologists, historians, professors, journalists, writers, and Web masters some credit. Information is free when you're researching, but you don't take credit for it. By citing, you give a very important nod to the original source.

As you do your Internet investigation, use Handout 2.2, Satisfying Sandwich of Key Facts. Let's review that now.

Remember, here are your search questions. You will now choose one to answer.

- What did the ancient Romans value in their government?
- What did ancient Romans value in individuals?
- Why was Julius Caesar considered a hero?

Handout 2.2, Internet Investigation: Reaching Back to Rome

Essential Questions: What did the ancient Romans value in their government? What did ancient Romans value in individuals? Why was Julius Caesar considered a hero?

Directions:

1. Choose among the levels of challenge—A, B, or C. If you are unsure which level to select, check with the teacher.

2. Answer the questions by taking paraphrased, cited notes on key facts.

3. Write an outline of a satisfying sandwich short answer: (a) topic sentence that answers the research question; and (b) two to three paraphrased examples (key facts) from the research source followed by in-text, parenthetical citations.

Understanding the Republic
A. Search Question: What did the ancient Romans value in their government?

1. **KNOWLEDGE:** Visit

   http://www.bbc.co.uk/schools/primaryhistory/romans/city_of_rome/

   http://www.historyforkids.org/learn/romans/government/index.htm, and

   http://www.socialstudiesforkids.com/articles/worldhistory/intro ancientrome1.htm.

   a. What is a republic?

   b. From what type of government did the Roman republic grow?

2. **APPLICATION:** Visit

   http://www.bbc.co.uk/schools/primaryhistory/romans/city_of_rome and http://en.wikipedia.org/wiki/Roman_Republic

   a. How do we know the Rome of Julius Caesar's day was a republic?

3. **Challenge—ANALYSIS:** Ask your teacher for a good website to visit about American government. Compare the basic facts of the American republic to the ancient Roman republic.

Understanding Roman Values
B. Search Question: What did ancient Romans value in individuals?

1. **ANALYSIS:** Visit three or more of the sites listed.

   a. **Regarding suicide:**
      http://internetshakespeare.uvic.ca/Library/SLT/ideas/suicide1.html

continued on next page

  b. **Regarding Stoicism and Epicureanism:**
     http://internetshakespeare.uvic.ca/Library/SLT/history/brutus +1.html

  c. **Regarding stars and omens:**
     http://internetshakespeare.uvic.ca/Library/SLT/plays/stars.html

  d. **Ambition and other political values:**
     http://www.bbc.co.uk/history/ancient/romans/empire_01.shtml

  e. **Paradoxical values:**
     http://www.bbc.co.uk/history/ancient/romans/empire_01.shtml

Understanding Julius Caesar

C. Search Question: Why was Julius Caesar considered a hero?

  1. **ANALYSIS:** Visit three or more of the sites listed.

     http://ancienthistory.about.com/od/caesar1/a/Caesar_3.htm

     http://ancienthistory.about.com/od/caesar1/a/Caesar_2.htm

     http://ancienthistory.about.com/od/caesar1/a/Caesar.htm

     http://www.roman-empire.net/republic/caesar-index.html

     http://ancienthistory.about.com/cs/caesarjulius/a/caesartriumvir.htm

     http://ancienthistory.about.com/od/romehistory/ss/RomanEras_2.htm

     http://ancienthistory.about.com/library/bl/bl_pennellhistoryofrome33.htm

     http://ancienthistory.about.com/library/bl/bl_pennellhistoryofrome34.htm#XXXIV

     http://www.bbc.co.uk/history/historic_figures/caesar_julius.shtml

  2. **Bonus Search Question, A or B: EVALUATION:** Visit http://www.bbc.co.uk/schools/romans/invasion.shtml. Search question: How do you define the word "failure"? Would you consider this event in Julius Caesar's life a failure? Why or why not?

  3. **SYNTHESIS & EVALUATION:** Search question: If you were to write a new biography of Caesar in a timeline that highlights his most important political and leadership accomplishments, what would those accomplishments be? Identify your criteria for "important."

  4. **EVALUATION:** Search question: Which accomplishments of Caesar show the big ideas of *glory, caprice, deception,* and *power*? When you match an accomplishment to a big idea, make a statement that expresses "Caesar's Big Idea"—the essential understanding, or what we learn about that concept.

Handout 2.3, Satisfying Sandwich of Key Facts

Directions:

1. Choose a search question challenge—A, B, or C. Answer the question by taking paraphrased, cited notes on key facts that answer this question.

2. Write an outline of a satisfying sandwich short answer: (a) topic sentence that answers the research question; and (b) two to three paraphrased examples (key facts) from the research source with parenthetical citations. Write your topic sentence last.

3. **CLAP** to check that you **cited**, **looked** for answers to the question, **asked** the question throughout your research, and **paraphrased**.

SEARCH QUESTION: _____

TOPIC SENTENCE (ANSWER): _____

_____

_____

_____

PARAPHRASED KEY FACT #1: _____

_____

_____

CITATION: _____

_____

PARAPHRASED KEY FACT #2: _____

_____

_____

CITATION: _____

_____

PARAPHRASED KEY FACT #3: _____

_____

_____

CITATION: _____

_____

Handout 2.4A CR, Brooding Brutus

Background: By himself in his orchard,[1] Brutus considers Cassius's proposal in act 1, wondering whether Caesar should be assassinated.[2]

TEXT	ANNOTATION /TRANSLATION

It must be by his death.[3] And for my part

I know no personal cause to spurn at[4] him

But for the general.[5] He would be crown'd:

How that might change his nature, there's the question.

It is the bright day that brings forth the adder[6]

And that craves wary walking. Crown him that,[7]

And then I grant[8] we put a sting in him

That at his will he may do danger with.

Th'abuse of greatness is when it disjoins[9]

Remorse from power.

1. Orchard: Garden of trees
2. To be assassinated: To be murdered suddenly after secret plotting; being killed due to one's position as a political figure
3. It must be by his death: Caesar must be killed
4. Spurn at him: Kick against him
5. For the general: For the public good, the good of Rome
6. Adder: Poisonous snake
7. Crown him that: If he is crowned king
8. I grant: I agree (with Cassius)
9. Disjoins: Separates
10. Perplexed: Puzzled, unsure, full of uncertainty
11. Justify: Prove to be right and just

continued on next page

Directions: Answer these questions in complete sentences.

1. **GENERALIZATION:** Brutus is perplexed[10] as he tries to make the best decision for his country. Reread his speech aloud in a voice that is worried and confused.

2. **GENERAL TO SPECIFIC:** Brutus is trying to decide why Caesar must be killed. He finds at least two reasons. What are they?

3. **EVALUATION:** What is your opinion of Brutus's reasons for killing Caesar? Do his reasons justify[11] murder? Why or why not?

4. **GENERAL TO SPECIFIC:** Choose one of the following statements that you believe is true. (Note how these statements mention big ideas.) Prove this statement is true by: (a) copying a quotation from the passage and (b) circling key words or phrases from the quotation (and any other parts of the passage) that help you prove the statement is true. Look up definitions as needed.

   a. Brutus is worried that Caesar is too *ambitious*. (AMBITION)

   b. Caesar *appears* dangerous to Brutus. (APPEARANCE)

   c. Brutus is considering whether to join Cassius's *conspiracy*. (CONSPIRACY)

   d. Brutus is *fearful* of the possibility that Caesar could be dangerous. (FEAR)

QUOTATION (act ___, scene ___, verse(s) ___) _____

_____

_____

_____

_____

_____

5. **VOCABULARY PRACTICE:** Find three new words you have learned from this reading and use each one in a sentence. Your satisfying sentences should include specific examples and should use the word as the correct part of speech.

6. **ANALYSIS:** Take one of the big ideas from this passage—ambition, appearance, or conspiracy—and draw a picture that represents this idea. Choose one of these options:

   a. A picture of a person, place, or thing that is mentioned in the passage, that to you represents a big idea.

   b. A picture of a person, place, or thing that many people would know and that also represents this big idea.

   c. NOTE: Try to make the drawing very symbolic, meaning, the image speaks for itself and you don't have to explain anything.

continued on next page

However, if you feel uncomfortable with drawing, then write a two-sentence explanation below the drawing to clarify what you were trying to do.

Handout 2.4B CR, Brooding Brutus

Background: By himself in his orchard,[1] Brutus considers Cassius's words, wondering if Caesar should be assassinated.[2]

TEXT	ANNOTATION /TRANSLATION

It must be by his death.[3] And for my part

I know no personal cause to spurn at[4] him

But for the general.[5] He would be crown'd:

How that might change his nature, there's the question.

It is the bright day that brings forth the adder[6]

And that craves wary walking. Crown him that,[7]

And then I grant[8] we put a sting in him

That at his will he may do danger with.

Th'abuse of greatness is when it disjoins[9]

Remorse from power. And to speak truth of Caesar,

I have not known when his affections sway'd

More than his reason. But 'tis a common proof

That lowliness is young ambition's ladder,

Whereto the climber-upward turns his face;

But when he once attains the upmost round

He then unto[10] the ladder turns his back,

Looks in the clouds, scorning[11] the base[12] degrees[13]

By which he did ascend.[14] So Caesar may.

continued on next page

1. Orchard: Garden of trees
2. To be assassinated: To be murdered suddenly after secret plotting; being killed due to one's position as a political figure
3. It must be by his death: Caesar must be killed
4. Spurn at him: Kick against him
5. For the general: For the public good, the good of Rome
6. Adder: Poisonous snake
7. Crown him that: If he is crowned king
8. I grant: I agree (with Cassius)
9. Disjoins: Separates
10. Unto: To
11. Scorning: Reject, dismiss, show dislike of
12. Base: Lower
13. Degrees: Rungs, steps
14. Ascend: Rise, move up from a lower place
15. Perplexed: Puzzled, unsure, full of uncertainty
16. Justify: Prove to be right and just

Directions: Answer these questions in complete sentences.

1. **GENERALIZATION:** Brutus is perplexed[15] as he tries to make the best decision for his country. Reread his speech aloud in a voice that is worried and confused.

2. **GENERAL TO SPECIFIC:** Brutus is trying to decide why Caesar must be killed. He finds three reasons. What are they?

3. **EVALUATION:** What is your opinion of Brutus's reasons for killing Caesar? Do his reasons justify[16] murder? Why or why not?

4. **GENERAL TO SPECIFIC:** Choose one of the following statements that you believe is true. (Note how these statements mention big ideas.) Prove this statement is true by (a) copying a quotation from the passage; (b) circling key words or phrases from the quotation and the passage that help you prove the statement is true; and (c) writing commentary—an explanation—of how the key words prove your statement is true. Look up definitions as needed.

   a. Brutus is worried that Caesar is too *ambitious*. (AMBITION)

   b. Caesar *appears* dangerous to Brutus. (APPEARANCE)

   c. Brutus is considering whether to join Cassius's *conspiracy*. (CONSPIRACY)

   d. Brutus is *fearful* of the possibility that Caesar could be dangerous. (FEAR)

   e. Cassius might have *persuaded* Brutus to *mistrust* Caesar. (PERSUASION, TRUST)

continued on next page

f. Brutus may be *deceiving* himself that Caesar is dangerous. (DECEPTION)

g. Brutus is thinking about his country as a good *patriot* would. (PATRIOTISM)

QUOTATION (act ___, scene ___, verse(s) ___) _____

_____

_____

_____

COMMENTARY: _____

_____

_____

_____

5. **DIGGING DEEPER INTO LANGUAGE:** Brutus draws an analogy between Caesar and an adder. He uses a metaphor: comparing two unlike things to each other to show an interesting connection. It is an equation: CAESAR = ADDER. Explore this metaphor by starting a word family.

    a. Find any key words from the passage in the same family as *adder*.

    b. Go to the thesaurus and find words similar to *adder* that could describe the feeling Brutus has. Record any other words that are your guesses about the connections you see Brutus making between Caesar and an adder.

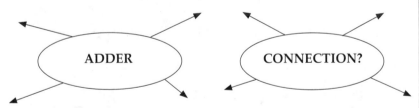

6. **GENERALIZATION:** Write a topic sentence to describe Brutus's feelings about Caesar using your key words and words from the word family. You will need to use adjectives to fill in the blanks below.

Brutus considers Caesar to be an adder because he believes Caesar is

_____, _____, and _____.

Handout 2.4C CR, Brooding Brutus

Background: By himself in his orchard, Brutus considers Cassius's words, wondering if Caesar should be assassinated.

TEXT   ANNOTATION /TRANSLATION

It must be by his death.[1] And for my part

I know no personal cause to spurn at him

But for the general.[2] He would be crown'd:

How that might change his nature, there's the question.

It is the bright day that brings forth the adder

And that craves wary walking. Crown him that,[3]

And then I grant we put a sting in him

That at his will he may do danger with.

Th'abuse of greatness is when it disjoins[4]

Remorse from power. And to speak truth of Caesar,

I have not known when his affections sway'd

More than his reason. But 'tis a common proof

That lowliness is young ambition's ladder,

Whereto the climber-upward turns his face;

But when he once attains the upmost round

He then unto the ladder turns his back,

Looks in the clouds, scorning the base degrees

By which he did ascend. So Caesar may.

Then lest he may, prevent. And since the quarrel

continued on next page

TEXT	ANNOTATION /TRANSLATION

Will bear no colour for the thing he is,

Fashion it thus; that what he is, augmented,

Would run to these and these extremities.

And therefore think him as a serpent's egg

(Which, hatch'd, would as his kind grow mischievous)

And kill him in the shell.

1. It must be by his death: Caesar must be killed

2. For the general: For the public good, the good of Rome

3. Crown him that: If he is crowned king

4. Disjoins: Separates

Directions: Answer these questions in complete sentences.

1. **GENERAL TO SPECIFIC:** Brutus is trying to decide why Caesar must be killed. He finds three reasons. What are they?

2. **EVALUATION:** What is your opinion of Brutus's reasons for killing Caesar? Do his reasons justify murder? Why or why not?

3. **GENERAL TO SPECIFIC:** Create a big idea statement (a topic sentence) that (a) draws a conclusion about how a big idea is present in this speech and (b) is provable with evidence. To prove each statement true, copy a quotation from the passage and comment using key words to prove your statement true. (Suggested big ideas: ambition, appearance, fear, persuasion, trust, deception, and patriotism).

TOPIC SENTENCE: _____

_____

_____

QUOTATION (act ___, scene ___, verse(s) ____) _____

_____

_____

_____

continued on next page

COMMENTARY: _____

_____

_____

_____

4. **DIGGING DEEPER INTO LANGUAGE:** Find the two instances of figurative language that Brutus uses to describe his concerns about Caesar. Identify key words (in this case, nouns that express concrete images—figurative language) and explore their connotations.

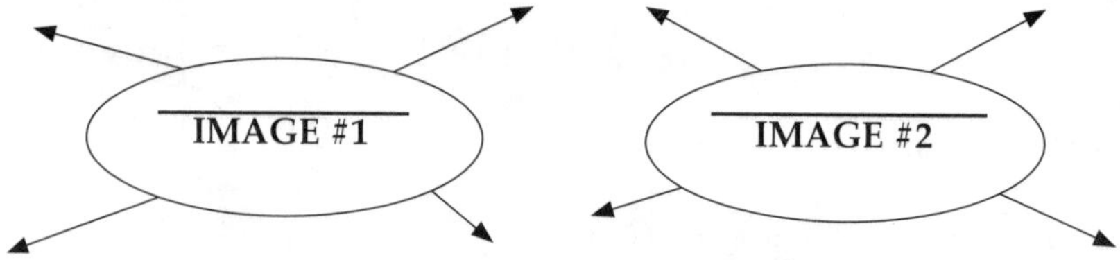

        IMAGE #1   IMAGE #2

5. **GENERALIZATION:** Write a topic sentence to describe Brutus's feelings about Caesar using one of these images. You will need to use two or three adjectives to fill in the blanks.

Brutus uses the image of _____ because he believes Caesar is
_____, _____, and _____.

Teaching Julius Caesar: *A Differentiated Approach* © 2010 Lyn Fairchild Hawks.

Handout 2.4D CR, Brooding Brutus

Background: By himself in his orchard, Brutus considers Cassius's words, wondering if Caesar should be assassinated.

TEXT	ANNOTATION /TRANSLATION

It must be by his death.[1] And for my part

I know no personal cause to spurn at him

But for the general.[2] He would be crown'd:

How that might change his nature, there's the question.

It is the bright day that brings forth the adder

And that craves wary walking. Crown him that,[3]

And then I grant we put a sting in him

That at his will he may do danger with.

Th'abuse of greatness is when it disjoins

Remorse from power. And to speak truth of Caesar,

I have not known when his affections sway'd

More than his reason. But 'tis a common proof

That lowliness is young ambition's ladder,

Whereto the climber-upward turns his face;

But when he once attains the upmost round

He then unto the ladder turns his back,

Looks in the clouds, scorning the base degrees

By which he did ascend. So Caesar may.

continued on next page

TEXT	ANNOTATION /TRANSLATION

Then lest he may, prevent. And since the quarrel

Will bear no colour for the thing he is,

Fashion it thus; that what he is, augmented,

Would run to these and these extremities.

And therefore think him as a serpent's egg

(Which, hatch'd, would as his kind grow mischievous)

And kill him in the shell.

1. It must be by his death: Caesar must be killed
2. For the general: For the public good, the good of Rome
3. Crown him that: If he is crowned king
4. Soliloquy: A dramatic monologue in which a character shares thoughts, for the audience's hearing only

Directions: Answer these questions in complete sentences and with evidence (paraphrases and direct quotations) from the play.

1. **ANALYSIS:** Brutus's soliloquy[4] is a search for justifications for assassinations. How would you classify his logic? Is it substantive or faulty—or both? Explain your labeling of his reasons.

2. **ANALYSIS:** We know that Cassius sparked this mental wrestling match for Brutus. How does knowing that Cassius is the cause of this deliberation influence your interpretation of Brutus's dilemma? Do you think Brutus is too easily influenced, and if so, by what? Or do you think Brutus is responding to legitimate concerns raised by Cassius? Return to act 1, scenes 2 and 3, and evaluate (a) Cassius's reasoning for assassination (spoken directly to Brutus) and (b) Cassius's soliloquy about his method (spoken in private).

3. **EVALUATION:** Are Brutus's assessments of Caesar's character accurate, in your estimation? (Note two instances of figurative language Brutus uses to characterize Caesar.) Use any evidence you have seen thus far in act 1 and 2 that either confirms or denies Brutus's interpretation of Caesar.

4. **ANALYSIS:** Through soliloquy, we are granted a window into Brutus's mind and heart. What is at work in his conscience? How do you know?

continued on next page

5. **ANALYSIS:** Caesar's character is never granted a soliloquy. Why? If the play is called *Julius Caesar*, why not give us interior monologue? What questions or issues does Shakespeare's choice raise?

6. **DIGGING DEEPER INTO LANGUAGE:** Where in the soliloquy does Shakespeare break the rhythm of iambic pentameter? What receives attention and emphasis? Why?

7. **ANALYSIS:** Read the second scene 2 soliloquy that follows this one, beginning with "'Brutus, thou sleep'st . . . " and that ends with " . . . at the hand of Brutus." How does Brutus's second round of private words confirm your prior interpretation of his character or make his character appear more complex?

8. **ANALYSIS:** Write a brief characterization of Brutus. Use key words and the emphasis provided by iambic pentameter to prove at least two of the six aspects of his character, including beliefs/thoughts/values. Make sure your characterization includes one or more topic sentences, at least three examples, and commentary on each example.

Teaching Julius Caesar: *A Differentiated Approach* © 2010 Lyn Fairchild Hawks.

Reading Act 2

Act 2 is an excellent time to increase reading confidence by helping students own the process. Mary Ellen Dakin's Chapter 9 in *Reading Shakespeare with Young Adults* offers excellent guidance with her literature circle corporations. Students play the roles of connector, summarizer, clarifier, questioner, wordsmith, prophet, character captain, vocabularian, illustrator, and literary luminary.

Continue to adapt CRs to your students' needs and to address learning goals. Act 2 provides an opportunity for students to take charge of the big ideas by encouraging them to increase the list found on Handout 1.6 and Handout 1.7. You can also use the Let's Make a Motif Motto mini-lesson on page 133 if you would like to distinguish between big ideas, motifs, and essential understandings (themes). With each new big idea and motif discovered, recommend that students return to act 1 to see if these concepts and elements appear even earlier. Some other tips:

- Since the goal is comprehension and interpretation rather than coverage, remember to keep CRs to a brief amount of text. With each new act of the play, you can increase the number of verses for each readiness level, as several of these suggested passages do, but keep passages under seventy-five lines. The focus should be translation, annotation, and critical thinking questions.

- You may choose to give different passages to different readiness levels (see suggested labels for each) and then have different TR groups present their answers to the CR questions to the class. Such a WCA jigsaw activity can help you review longer scenes such as act 2, scene 1, with the whole class.

- Here is a suggested lesson flow: TR groups complete CRs on various parts of the scene, then report back in a WCA. Each group presents on a particular literary device or concept, such as motifs or iambic pentameter. Your role is to help students link all these reports to big ideas. End class with a film viewing and discuss how directors and actors translate big ideas into blocking, staging, acting, camera angles, costuming, and scenery.

- When students find new big ideas, remind them to make connections with others to form word families. Flattery can be connected to big ideas of *persuasion, manipulation, conspiracy, glory, love,* and *loyalty*. Distinctions can be made between the word family of ancestry/history, from which such words as *leaders, influence,* and *impact on Rome* might be generated, versus ancestry/lineage, from which words such as *genealogy, forebears, role models,* and *good stock* might be generated. Such discussions help students see the nuances of language, the importance of perspective, the variety of interpretations available, the connectedness of ideas, and the importance of precision when writing topic sentences and thesis statements later. You are building word banks so that students can have greater choices when forming generalizations about complex ideas.

Suggested Passages for CRs

- **Brutus, scene 1 (ELL/NOV):** "'Brutus, thou sleep'st. . . . Thy full petition at the hand of Brutus." (Big ideas: ancestry/history, appearance, conspiracy, deception, honor, indecision, love, loyalty, nobility, manipulation, patriotism, persuasion, revenge. Motif: sleep.)

- **Lucius and Brutus, scene 1 (ELL/NOV):** "No, sir, their hats are pluck'd. . . . To hide thee from prevention." (Big ideas: appearance, conspiracy, cowardice, deception, evil, honesty, monstrosity, nature, realism. Motifs: clothing/cloaks/mantles, night/darkness, images from classical mythology.)

- **Decius, Cinna, Casca, Brutus, Cassius, scene 1 (OT/ADV):** "Here lies the east. . . . Of any promise that hath pass'd from him." (Big ideas: appearance, bond/oath, conspiracy, courage, frailty, honesty, idealism, loyalty, nature, nobility, patriotism, virtue/goodness. Motifs: light/day/sun/East, fire, blood.)

> The 1970 version of *Julius Caesar* (with Charlton Heston, Jason Robards, and Sir John Gielgud) has Casca pointing his sword at Brutus as "the sun" that "arises."

- **Decius, Cassius, Brutus, Trebonius, scene 1 (OT/ADV):** "Shall no man else . . . he will live and laugh at this hereafter." (Big ideas: conspiracy, envy, fear, idealism, love, loyalty, realism, wrath/rage. Motifs: blood, body.)

- **Cassius and Decius, scene 1 (ELL/NOV):** "But it is doubtful yet . . . I will bring him to the Capitol." (Big ideas: conspiracy, fate, fear, flattery, manipulation, nature, persuasion. Motifs: lions, dreams, night.)

Fate in Shakespeare's time referred to fortune or forces of the universe, a spinning wheel that brought a person from top to bottom or vice versa. Since rise or ruin for any person is never a given, Renaissance thinking began to confront that reality: Is there really an order or a chain of being? If the plague can kill the rich and thus provide opportunity for the poor to acquire land, what does that mean? Or does nature revolt at the signs of natural order being overturned? *Julius Caesar* shows the caprice of fortune vis-à-vis the natural order, for Caesar, the hero and a ruler, seems fated to die, while nature revolts at the conspiracy and then the tragedy. The ambiguity of Shakespeare's perspective reflects the fluidity of the time, when the exchange of new ideas accelerated through print and travel, when new religions formed, and when "new" lands were discovered (Dye n. pag.).

- **Metellus, Brutus, Cassius, scene 1 (ELL/NOV)**: "Caius Ligarius. . . . Therefore thou sleep'st so sound." (Big ideas: constancy, loyalty, nature, patriotism, persuasion, revenge, wrath/rage. Motifs: morning/day, sleep.)
- **Portia and Brutus, scene 1 (OT/ADV)**: "Dear my lord. . . . Render me worthy of this noble wife!" (Big ideas: ancestry/lineage, bond/oath, constancy, courage, fear, honesty, honor, love, loyalty, nature, nobility, patience, reputation, right, secrecy, virtue/goodness. Motifs: sickness/health, night, blood, male/female.)

Fate and free will ride a seesaw together in Shakespeare's plays. His rich yet ambiguous presentations (are the characters choosing or are they pawns of fateful coincidence?) again may rise from the fact that his era was rather "cuspy"—both medieval and what we know as "modern." The idea of choice and personal responsibility seemed unlikely if God and monarchy were supreme, and Elizabethans knew the danger of questioning God or government. The mystical view of one's body and soul being a microcosm of God's natural order of the universe reigned. Yet the arts and sciences were experiencing tremendous surges of creativity, as Renaissance thinkers exerted more independence than in prior eras (Dye n. pag.).

- **Calpurnia and Caesar, scene 2 (ELL/NOV):** "What mean you, Caesar. . . . Will come when it will come." (Big ideas: chaos, courage, cowardice, fate, free will, love, loyalty, nature, prophecy/augury, realism, royalty/hierarchy. Motifs: lions, blood, dead/ghosts, images from classical mythology.)

Death as a big idea hovers over every scene. Roman and Elizabethan attitudes toward death can be explored alongside love, loyalty, patriotism, and revenge.

- **Servant, Calpurnia, and Caesar, scene 2 (ELL/NOV):** "They would not have you. . . . I will stay at home." (Big ideas: courage, confidence/pride, cowardice, fate, fear, frailty, free will, honesty, nature, prophecy/augury. Motifs: animals, lions, health.)
- **Caesar, Calpurnia, Decius, scene 2 (OT/ADV):** (Big ideas: caprice, confidence/pride, conspiracy, courage, cowardice, fate, fear, flattery, free will, honesty, love, loyalty, manipulation, persuasion, royalty/hierarchy. Motifs: dreams, blood, male/female.)

Sample Mini-Lesson: Writing Instruction: Pin the Tail on the Donkey Character Analysis

Materials Needed

- Names or images of the four protagonists posted: Caesar, Antony, Brutus, and Cassius
- Big ideas list posted
- Handout 2.5, Topical Subgroups and Significant Particulars Chart (page 138)
- Index cards and markers
- Text of *Julius Caesar* for each student

Explain: Writing a character analysis involves several critical thinking steps because characters are complex. Remember how you analyzed your own character, looking at six different aspects? No doubt you barely scratched the surface of who you are, because you have many qualities. **Direct:** What were those six aspects? Write them in your notes, and then let's share.
Explain: Here we have the names of the four protagonists of *Julius Caesar* posted. In this mini-lesson, we are going to probe the catacombs of their

personalities to figure out who they are. Catacombs, or underground burial grounds and passageways beneath the city of Rome, date back to the post-Caesar era of the 2nd century A.D.

Direct: With a partner, triad, or quad, discuss the personality of the protagonist assigned to you. (Arrange it so that each character has at least two groups analyzing him.) Your tasks:

- Identify the six aspects of that character as demonstrated in acts 1 and 2. Write down at least three examples from your memory of the character's speech, actions, thoughts, etc.

- Find at least two adjectives for that character based on these details. These adjectives should connect to big ideas. In other words, adjectives such as "friendly" or "mean" or "nice" won't cut it! Use the big ideas list posted here to choose adjectives that will give your analysis some depth. Choose at least two if not three adjectives.

- From act 1 or act 2, find two quotations for each adjective proving each is an accurate description. You can always change your adjectives if you can't find quotations to support. Write your adjectives in big letters on the index cards I give you. Be prepared to share your adjectives and quotations aloud with the class.

- Let's pin the tail on these donkeys. We will ask each group to send a representative up to pin an adjective on characters. Then each group should defend their descriptive adjective using quotations.

- Let's discuss:

  - Which adjective seems most apt?

  - Which adjectives are in the same word family (are synonyms)?

  - Are there any contradictory qualities we are naming—or aren't naming—such as honesty mixed with dishonesty or self-deception (Brutus), or a balance of realism and idealism (Cassius)? Constancy mixed with malleability (Caesar)?

  - Do some characters show an excess of one quality over another? (For example, Brutus's idealism.) Remember that Shakespeare presents us with complex individuals, not caricatures.

- Choose your favorite character of these four and complete the following brainstorming exercise independently. You will choose your favorite adjectives, which we will now call topical subgroups (Benthall 33), and the most substantive details, which we will call significant particulars (Benthall 19).

- We call the descriptive adjectives topical subgroups because they are the summative, grouping, describing words
we need to form topic sentences. They are the forest that
contains the trees, which are the details and examples.

- We call the details significant particulars because they are
the best details in the right order. That's ultimately what
you want in a good essay—right words in the right order.
You don't want just any old details, whatever quotations
you see first or paraphrases you can throw together, but
the ones that are most important, interesting, and significant—details you can comment on. Otherwise, your essay
would be nothing but a grocery list of details, rather than
a convincing argument, and who wants to read a grocery
list?

- Create the same chart I have posted (Handout 2.5, Topical
Subgroups & Significant Particulars Chart) and brainstorm
information for each of the two columns. Choose three adjectives for the topical subgroups column and find nine significant
particulars—three for each topical subgroup—in your text. Finish by writing a topic sentence. You may work alone or with a
partner.

The three-adjective formula modeled here for these practice topic
sentences is just that, a formula. You can also offer students two levels
with models—the Challenge #1 and Challenge #2 level. Challenge
#1 topic sentence: Brutus is patriotic, idealistic, and confused. Chal-
lenge #2 topic sentence: Brutus's idealism confuses his loyalty. Note
how #2 uses a higher level of analysis, cause and effect, to share a
deeper essential understanding, or theme. Another Challenge #2 topic
sentence: Cassius's realism is often in conflict with Brutus's idealism
and is the reason their political plans for a new order do not succeed.
In this example, a higher level of analysis—comparison—is merged
with cause and effect.

- Let's share our topic sentences with everyone and defend our
statements using our examples.

Alternate Approach to Pin the Tail on the Donkey Lesson

This lesson relies heavily on verbal-linguistic abilities. The options access other learning styles while reinforcing the understanding that characters are complex and can be viewed and interrogated from many angles.

Kinesthetic Activity: Firing Line. Divide students into MR groups and ask each to use notes from Handout 2.5, Topical Subgroups and Significant Particulars Chart to create a TV interview in which the character faces a press room. Journalists will ask the character whether it's true he is responsible for certain actions and outcomes and whether he possesses certain personality traits. Directions: (a) Create a skit in which (1) someone plays the character, (2) others play supportive and antagonist reporters, and (3) someone plays the host and moderator; (b) The scene should illustrate the positive and negative aspects of this character as he sits beneath the hot lamp of journalistic scrutiny; (c) Bonus given to skits that use Shakespearean vocabulary in all speaking; (d) Present skits. Audience members can gain bonus credit for asking text-based questions and should analyze how well groups presented character aspects using quotations and performance techniques.

Visual-Spatial Activity: Metaphor Making. Divide students into MR groups and ask students to use their notes from Handout 2.5 to develop a metaphor to represent their character. Students should use their topical subgroups to identify an animal, object, or place that could represent their character. (Examples: Brutus is a battered rock in a storm. Cassius is a rattlesnake.) Each group must complete a visual (poster, slide show, or webpage) showing the three topical subgroups defended with quotations. Challenge level: integrate all topical subgroups and significant particulars into the illustration (a snake's tongue or tail might also serve as quotations). When groups present, the class can discuss (a) whether the metaphor is inherently negative or positive and (b) whether other metaphors could apply.

Sample Mini-Lesson: Let's Make a Motif Motto

Materials Needed

- Poster paper and markers or student access to a interactive white board for electronic posting

Direct: Today we're going to explore a literary device called a motif. To get started, draw or write the key words or images from what I am about to explain.

Explain: In act 1 we saw how nature exploded into chaos right after Cassius and other senators began to conspire against Caesar. We saw lightning, lions walking the streets, and other troubling signs, such as fire and people running in panic. Images of nature in *Julius Caesar* are a literary device called a motif, which is a repeated symbol in a literary work that is often a sensory, physical, concrete image. Motifs carry big ideas on their backs. Let's take the American flag: what big ideas does the flag represent? What about the rose you give someone on Valentine's Day? If these images appear frequently in a work of literature, they can act as motifs, carrying the concepts of freedom and patriotism or love and romance.

Direct: What key words did you hear in this definition? (Students should note words such as *repeated*, *symbol*, *sensory*, and *concrete*.)

Explain: Here are some motifs from acts 1 and 2. Do you remember where these appeared?

a. Clothing (1.1, 1.2, 2.1, 2.2)

b. Blood (1.1, 1.3, 2.1)

c. Metal (1.1, 1.2, 1.3, 2.1)

d. Sickness (1.2, 2.1)

e. Stars (1.2, 2.1, 2.2)

f. Storms (1.3, 2.1)

g. Night/darkness (1.3, 2.1)

h. Ghosts (1.3, 2.1, 2.2)

i. Money (2.1)

j. Lions (1.3, 2.1, 2.2)

k. Male/female (1.3, 2.1, 2.4)

l. Day/light (2.1)

Direct:

1. In a minute you will turn to a partner and flip through act 1 and 2 to search for quotations with these motifs.

   a. First, generate a word family of at least five synonyms. (A motif of "stars" might lead to a word family that includes starry, planets, comets, and meteors, while storms might lead to clouds, lightning, thunder, and so forth. With online text, students can use a search function to find these words and their synonyms.)

   b. Once you have two quotations, post it for the class. Underline or highlight the key words that carry big ideas. (Consider the option of blogs, Twitter, wikis, and other online postings for this activity.)

Explain: Motifs are eggs you can crack to get at the big idea, which we'll think of as the yolk inside—the place that is most fertile and most nutritious. But to understand the egg, you need to know the hen and the henhouse. You need to know what produced the egg. And that's the culture that surrounds the motif.

Direct: Let's choose one pair's quotation to analyze.

1. Name the motif this quotation represents. (Students who posted it should stay silent.)

2. What associations do we have in our culture with this motif? (For example, clothing covers nakedness; clothing is fashion and style; clothing is status; and so forth.)

3. What expressions, such as idioms, proverbs, mottos, and figurative language ("The clothes make the man") or allusions ("The emperor's new clothes") do we have with this motif?

4. Let's create a motto for some motifs. Use a formula of an equation (such as a metaphor) or the verb *means*. Fill in the blanks: Blood equals/means _____. Storms = _____. This is a motif motto: the short version of an essential understanding, or a theme.

Direct: Choose one of the following challenges:

1. A-Level Challenge: Look for the motif of sleep/dreams and find quotations.

   a. Discuss what connotations such words have by building a word family.

   b. Are these associations positive or negative?

   c. What are our culture's idioms, proverbs, mottos, figurative language, and allusions with this motif? (Think of expressions family or friends have.)

        d. Create a motif motto for sleep/dreams.

2. B-Level Challenge: Look for new motifs we have not yet discussed. Look for important nouns, verbs, adjectives, and adverbs—key words—that create images for us as readers.

        a. To clarify the motif, identify connotations by building a word family.

        b. Look at our culture's associations with this motif (idioms, proverbs, mottos, figurative language, allusions).

        c. Research Elizabethan culture's associations with this motif.

        d. Create a motif motto, a sentence of more than ten words, that uses cause and effect or figurative language (metaphor, simile, analogy, or personification) to express an essential understanding (theme).

Direct: As you continue to read the play, look for these motifs as you annotate and keep an eye out for new ones.

Design Tips: Performance Lessons

How are your students doing at performance? Performance should be about celebration of excellent drama and comprehension of big ideas; therefore, certain guidelines and routines should be in place. Here are some quick tips for designing performance lessons.

- *Clarify the skill goal.* If students are to present a scene, whether as a WCA or group activity, what is the purpose? Is the goal for you to model tips for translation and students to practice? A WCA choral reading or brief scene performance by a few students to the whole class, peers directing, could help meet that goal. Or do students need to work in TR groups in order to have enough individual practice time using tips for translation? Perhaps the goal is to explore aspects of characterization, plot, or figurative language; perhaps particular scenes can be practiced in MR groups, then presented and analyzed in a WCA to explore the same concept. Develop a clear rubric of English language arts skills to focus the performance activity.

- *Review the rubric with students, and use it to guide feedback.* In the act 1 chapter, you saw a model of a rubric on Handout 1.6, Recitation Regulars (visit http://www.lynhawks.com). When developing a new performance activity, decide which performance elements are most essential to measure: enunciation, poise, blocking, motivation, volume, etc. Use this rubric to guide the discussion after each performance. See page 137 for another sample.

Books with tips for classroom management and community building include *The First Days of School: How to Be an Effective Teacher, Differentiating Instruction in the Regular Classroom,* and *The Compassionate Classroom: Lessons that Nurture Wisdom and Empathy.*

- *Establish expectations about a supportive classroom community.* Actors need to feel safe in order to take risks. If you haven't already created a classroom contract or established the golden rule for performance activities, try ACTS: A = Attention (no talking during performances); C = Compliments (tell performers what's working); T = Tact (help performers with constructive criticism); and S = Specificity (give detailed feedback, not abstract adjectives and nouns).

- *Keep the text short and the creativity long.* You don't need much Shakespeare text to get a great scene. Assign groups small excerpts (scenelets) and help them see the range of choices for acting, staging, costuming, props, and scenery. One effective activity applicable to many scenes is cue cards, which are adjectives to inspire a variety of readings of particular characters, and motive matchsticks, which are abstract nouns (big ideas) to help students try different character motivations and see the possible plot consequences and greater thematic picture. These activities can inspire close reading so students can determine which cue or motive is most apropos to the text, and you can use these discussions to help students see when they are developing interpretations that are too thin versus those that are truly grounded in textual evidence. See pages 139 and 141 for samples.

Cue cards and motive matchsticks (see pages 139 and 141) make good homework and can be integrated with CRs. Encourage students to find a quiet, private space (even if it needs to be the bathroom) to practice reading aloud.

- *Shakespeare Set Free* is an excellent series offering a great choice of performance activities.
- Use Handout 2.6, Lesson Creation Template (see http://www.lynhawks.com) to develop your own act 2 performance lesson.

Performance Rubric

1. **Acting:** Effort and quality of acting when not speaking; presence on stage.

    NOVICE   ON-TARGET   ADVANCED

2. **Acting:** Creativity in two or more areas:

    A. Expression of motivation

    B. Gestures and movement

    C. Facial expressions

    D. Volume

    E. Pacing

    NOVICE   ON-TARGET   ADVANCED

3. **Blocking and Direction:** Balance of actors on stage, movement across stage; use of full space.

    NOVICE   ON-TARGET   ADVANCED

4. **Big Ideas and Themes:** Use of acting and blocking to represent a big idea.

    NOVICE   ON-TARGET   ADVANCED

5. **Flow, Unity, and Preparedness:**

    A. Evidence that the group has practiced several times.

    B. Evidence that the group is working as a team.

    NOVICE   ON-TARGET   ADVANCED

Comments:

Handout 2.5, Topical Subgroups & Significant Particulars Chart	
TOPICAL SUBGROUPS	**SIGNIFICANT PARTICULARS**
#1: _____	Quotation or Paraphrase #1: _____ _____ _____(act __, scene __, lines ____) Quotation or Paraphrase #2: _____ _____ _____(act __, scene __, lines ____) Quotation or Paraphrase #3: _____ _____ _____(act __, scene __, lines ____)
#2: _____	Quotation or Paraphrase #1: _____ _____ _____(act __, scene __, lines ____) Quotation or Paraphrase #2: _____ _____ _____(act __, scene __, lines ____) Quotation or Paraphrase #3: _____ _____ _____(act __, scene __, lines ____)
#3: _____	Quotation or Paraphrase #1: _____ _____ _____(act __, scene __, lines ____) Quotation or Paraphrase #2: _____ _____ _____(act __, scene __, lines ____) Quotation or Paraphrase #3: _____ _____ _____(act __, scene __, lines ____)

_____ is _____, _____, and _____.
(character name)   (topical subgroup #1) (topical subgroup #2)   (topical subgroup #3)

Teaching Julius Caesar: *A Differentiated Approach* © 2010 Lyn Fairchild Hawks.

Handout 2.7, Cue Cards

Directions:

Use cue cards when you act a character in *Julius Caesar.* Cue cards offer suggestions for your:

- Tone of voice (emotional attitude)
- Facial expressions
- Gestures, movements, and use of space (a character's physical presence)
- Volume of voice (loudness or softness)
- Pace (speed of delivery; pauses; timing in relation to other actors)
- Emphasis (stress on particular words or syllables)

ALOOF: Read this character in a cold, distant tone of voice, as if you feel disconnected from others or even superior to them.

INSISTENT: Read this character in a pushy, persistent[1] tone of voice to get what you want.

IRATE: Read this character in an angry tone of voice, as if you are fuming[2] about something.

LOVING: Read this character in an affectionate tone of voice, as if you care deeply for those with whom you are speaking.

SELFISH: Read this character in a childish, demanding tone of voice, as if you deserve all you desire and will become upset if you don't get it.

SOLEMN: Read this character in a serious tone of voice, as if the topic you are discussing is very important, perhaps even worrisome[3] or sad.

DEPRESSED: Read this character in a sad tone of voice, as if you have little energy or hope.

JOVIAL: Read this character in a fun-loving, joking tone, as if everything amuses you and you have a positive attitude.

continued on next page

Choose two of the following options for your acting. Look up the adjective and define it in terms of how an actor will behave: fearful, passionate, envious, curious, excited.

1. Persistent: Trying even though there are obstacles; not taking "no" for an answer; tenacious

2. Fuming: Angry; frustrated; on the point of exploding

3. Worrisome: Troubling, worrying

Handout 2.8, Motive Matchsticks

The spark to character action, or the catalyst, is often a motive.

Directions:

1. Read your assigned scene and try different motives for various statements by a character.

2. Decide which motive makes the most sense. Use key words from the character's statements to defend your decision. Identify a new motive if you find one in the text not listed here.

MOTIVE OPTION #1:
LOYALTY

- What is this character loyal to?
- Why?
- What key words show loyalty?

MOTIVE OPTION #2:
ENVY

- What is this character envious of?
- Why?
- What key words show envy?

MOTIVE OPTION #3:
AMBITION

- What are this character's ambitions?
- Why?
- What key words show envy?

MOTIVE OPTION #4:
FEAR

- What does this character fear?
- Why?
- What key words show fear?

MOTIVE OPTION #5:
IDEALISM

- What are this character's ideals?
- Why?
- What key words show idealism?

MOTIVE OPTION #6:
LOVE

- Who or what does this character love?
- Why?
- What key words show love?

MOTIVE OPTION #7:
REVENGE

- What does this character wish to avenge?
- Why?
- What key words show the desire for revenge?

Handout 2.9, Act 2 Quiz

Name_____ Period_____

1. The messages that Cassius arranges to be tossed into Brutus's home tell Brutus to:

   a. Find Cassius as soon as possible in order to plot.

   b. "Speak" and reform Rome.

   c. Be "loyal" to Caesar because he is Rome's leader.

   d. Beware of Antony because he's "disloyal."

2. Brutus does not want the conspirators to:

   a. Swear an oath.

   b. Meet at night.

   c. Include him in the plot.

   d. Believe in soothsayers.

   e. Kill Caesar.

3. Cassius and Brutus disagree over:

   a. Whether they can trust one another.

   b. Where the dawn appears in the sky.

   c. Whether to include Caius Ligarius in the plot.

   d. Whether to kill Antony.

4. Decius insists he can get Caesar to appear at the Capitol because:

   a. Caesar can be flattered and manipulated.

   b. Caesar is afraid to stay at home due to prophecies.

   c. Decius is Caesar's favorite.

   d. Caesar wants to veto the senate's latest legislation.

5. Portia demands that Brutus:

   a. Share what makes him solemn and worried.

   b. Trust her good reputation.

   c. Trust that she won't share his secrets.

   d. All of the above.

   e. None of the above.

6. The scene between Caius Ligarius and Brutus shows that:

   a. Brutus has a noble reputation.

   b. The conspirators think Rome is sick and that Caesar's death will make Rome well.

   c. Brutus is suspicious of Cassius.

continued on next page

d. a and b

e. b and c

7. The scene between Calpurnia and Caesar presents the following big ideas:

    a. Fate and fear

    b. Loyalty and love

    c. Courage and cowardice

    d. Envy and chaos

    e. a, b, and c

    f. a, b, and d

8. Artemidorus hopes to:

    a. Find Portia to stop Brutus.

    b. Join the conspiracy and be its leader.

    c. Get a letter to Caesar to warn him.

    d. Stop Caesar and share the soothsayer's latest prophecy.

    e. Beat Antony in a race in order to gain Caesar's favor.

9. Translate the passage below into your own words.

    Decius: *This dream is all amiss interpreted,*

    It was a vision fair and fortunate.

    Your statue spouting blood in many pipes,

    In which so many smiling Romans bath'd,

    Signifies that from you great Rome shall suck

    Reviving blood . . ."

10. When, to whom, and why does Decius make this speech?

11. What are the big ideas expressed in these lines?

12. Write a satisfying sandwich paragraph (topic sentence, context, supporting details, and commentary) in response to either question:

    a. *Characterization.* Which character seems most likely to be the hero of the story right now: Julius Caesar, Brutus, Cassius, or Antony? Why?

    b. *Big ideas.* Which of these ideas seems the most important in light of the characters and events—conspiracy, fate, frailty, fear, deception, or love? Why?

Big Ideas in Act 2: Make Your Own Reference Guide

Identify big ideas most helpful to you and discussions with your students. Record quotations.

The Big Idea of _____ : act 1, scene ___, _____ : "_____ _____ _____."	*The Big Idea of* _____ : act 1, scene ___, _____ : "_____ _____ _____."
The Big Idea of _____ : act 1, scene ___, _____ : "_____ _____ _____."	*The Big Idea of* _____ : act 1, scene ___, _____ : "_____ _____ _____."
The Big Idea of _____ : act 1, scene ___, _____ : "_____ _____ _____."	*The Big Idea of* _____ : act 1, scene ___, _____ : "_____ _____ _____."
The Big Idea of _____ : act 1, scene ___, _____ : "_____ _____ _____."	*The Big Idea of* _____ : act 1, scene ___, _____ : "_____ _____ _____."

Act 3

Introduction

The Philosophy behind Act 3

Act 3 presents the play's crisis and other moments of great interest. Perform as much of act 3 as you can, and end classes with film clips and cinematic analysis. Continue to assign CRs for homework, allowing students increasing independence. Teach students the art of rhetoric and how to answer and pose analytical, evaluative questions that drive good discussion and writing. Lead Socratic discussions to help students explore the play and to develop answers to essential questions. These activities prepare students to not only choose essay topics and project options that interest them but also to hunt for evidence—details from the text—that will make their writing and presentations convincing and substantive.

What's in Store

In this chapter you will find:

- Mini-lessons on rhetoric and iambic pentameter;
- Suggested CR passages and questions;
- Options for performance and cinematic analysis lessons;
- Socratic questions—the essential questions to drive daily discussions, writing discussions, writing assignments, and projects; and
- Tiered writing assignments.

Companion Website

The scholar's seat: Examine the correspondence between Plutarch's *Lives* and *Julius Caesar*: a personal Internet investigation.

To access the companion website, visit http://www.lynhawks.com, click on Shakespeare's image, and log in with username (bard) and password (caesar). Go to the Act 3 section.

Suggested Calendar

This calendar is a sample guide for pacing lessons throughout the unit.

MONDAY	TUESDAY	WEDNESDAY	THURSDAY	FRIDAY
Introduce act 3. Perform scene 1. Homework: CR	TR, MR, or WCA: Perform excerpts of scene 2. Film clip. Homework: CR	TR, MR, or WCA: Perform Brutus's and Antony's speeches, scene 3. Film clip. Homework: CR	WCA: Mini-Lesson: *May the Best Speech Win* Homework: Rewrite persuasive paragraph	WCA: Mini-Lesson: *May the Best Speech Win*, continued Homework: Rewrite persuasive paragraph
TR, MR, or WCA: Scenelet doubling or cinematic analysis Homework: CR	TR, MR, or WCA: Scenelet doubling or cinematic analysis Homework: Notes for Socratic seminar	TR, MR, or WCA: Socratic seminar Homework: Choose essay prompt and begin notes	WCA: Mini-Lesson: *Five Stresses Are All You've Got* Homework: Study for quiz	Act 3 quiz

Sample Mini-Lesson: The Art of Rhetoric: May the Best Speech Win

Materials needed: Posted: "Romans, countrymen, and lovers" and "Friends, Romans, countrymen." You may also wish to post the entire speeches.

Explain: Politics is not just about making laws: it's also about winning elections and the favor of the people. What is one way politicians win? With words. In *Julius Caesar*, there's a battle not with bullets but with elegant and powerful speaking. Romans in Caesar's day valued and admired the art of rhetoric, also known as oratory and public speaking. Elizabethans with access to education studied these techniques, so they would have been familiar with Antony's and Brutus's tactics when giving Caesar's eulogies.

Direct: The question we'll explore is who had the better speech. This is an important question because after Caesar is murdered, the Roman citizens are screaming and clamoring in the streets. The people are outraged that Caesar is killed, and many want somebody's blood. There is chaos. The people must be calmed. Who will calm them? Antony and Brutus could do the job, but they are suddenly rivals. Why? Who or what are they rivals for? Turn to a partner to discuss. Let's share our answers.

> Show clips from films of the mob scene before Brutus speaks and his efforts to gain control. This viewing will help set the scene and establish the import of Antony's and Brutus's words that could make a big difference.

Explain: At the crisis of the play, two men stand before the Roman citizenry to make funeral speeches in honor of Caesar, and the question is, who will win the hearts of the people? Let's predict the answer by studying the first part of each of their speeches.

Direct: Let's read the following excerpts of their speeches dramatically. (Other options: have a talented student actor or speaker practice ahead of time and perform, or show clips of these lines from movie versions.)

- Brutus: "Romans, countrymen, and lovers . . . I pause for a reply."
- Antony: "Friends, Romans, countrymen . . . and I must pause till it come back to me."

Let's look at the art behind their speaking. Did you know there's rhetorical technique buried in a phrase of only three words? Brutus says, "Romans, countrymen, and lovers" and Antony says, "Friends, Romans, countrymen . . . "

Both use what is called tricolon: a phrase or statement of three balanced parts. Why does this make for effective speaking?

- Three is a magical number;
- Three's a charm, building to a climactic, third element;
- Three inspires us to clap (Maguire) or cheer, sing, or keep rhythm. Examples:
  - "Red, white, and blue" (patriotic American phrase);
  - "Liberté, egalité, fraternité" (motto of the French Revolution) (Maguire);
  - Idioms and proverbs such as "Lock, stock, and barrel," "Hook, line, and sinker," "Scrub, rinse, repeat," and "See no evil, hear no evil, speak no evil."

> Consider printing these out and asking various students to stand when you point at them and orate or sing their tricolon.

♦ Lincoln's second inaugural address, "with malice toward none, with charity toward all, with firmness in the right . . .";

♦ Barack Obama's inaugural address: "My fellow citizens: I stand here today humbled by the task before us, grateful for the trust you've bestowed, mindful of the sacrifices borne by our ancestors";

♦ "A-B-C, / Easy as 1, 2, 3 / Simple as do, re, mi . . ." ("ABC," 1970 song written by The Corporation and sung by The Jackson 5);

♦ "Doe, a deer, a female deer . . ." ("Do-Re-Mi" from Rodgers and Hammerstein's 1959 musical, *The Sound of Music*);

♦ "Signed, sealed, delivered . . ." ("Signed, Sealed, Delivered I'm Yours" by Stevie Wonder); and

♦ "*Veni, vidi, vici.*" ("I came, I saw, I conquered" spoken by Julius Caesar. Caesar's statement in his message to the Roman senate in 47 B.C. has been interpreted as a way of showing his power to a senate he did not respect and to express the complete rout that was his military victory.) (Maguire).

Can you think of other examples?

Let's examine: who said it better, Brutus or Antony? Look closely at the two tricolons. There are two key differences. What are they?

■ Difference #1: Antony leaves out the "and," the connective conjunction, a technique which is called *asyndeton* (Maguire). Why is that better? By leaving out what the audience expects to hear—the conjunction "and"—the speaker gets our attention. There is speed and urgency to what is being said.

■ Difference #2: Antony uses escalation by increasing the amount of syllables from monosyllabic ("Friends") to bisyllabic ("Romans") to trisyllabic ("countrymen"). The increasing rhythm carries listeners along.

Listen to the two openings again . . . how Brutus's slows down while Antony's speeds up. Speed increases our interest and perhaps even our heart rate. We expect something big.

So in round one, Antony wins. He's got punch (emphasis) and good pacing to his words, which gets our attention. Isn't that the aim of politicians when campaigning?

Direct: In the analysis you are about to complete, you will read aloud either Brutus's or Antony's words and dissect their techniques. You will make the judgment of who had the better speech overall. With a partner or a triad, you will do the following:

Since Brutus's speech is shorter, you may choose to give it to ELL/ NOV students. Consider dividing Handout 3.1, Rhetorical Techniques, (page 151) into several sections and giving TR partnerships or triads two techniques each to prepare. Gauge how difficult the rhetorical technique may be for students to grasp or to find, and distribute techniques accordingly.

1. Read the speech you are given aloud. Read it at least twice, with each person taking a turn to read all or part of it slowly and with feeling.

2. Using the information about rhetorical techniques given to you, find the line(s) in Brutus's or Antony's speech that match the definitions.

3. Practice saying the line from the play. Develop an explanation using the definition of how the rhetorical technique makes the line powerful. It's up to you to defend Brutus or Antony. If they don't speak well, an angry mob gets violent.

4. Let's present our analyses of various lines from the speeches. Let's argue for what has the most impact on us as listeners. Dissect how key words, stress on those words, pacing, and other factors get us to "lend" Brutus and Antony our "ears."

5. (Note that both speakers are masterful, but Antony's reliance on concrete imagery and emotional appeals wins the people's hearts.)

Homework Options

- Ask students to revise their persuasive paragraphs from the school meeting (pages 77 and 84) using three or more rhetorical devices.

- Ask students to examine how props—physical objects—add drama and help persuade the public during both Brutus's and Antony's speeches. By brainstorming the visual impact and symbolic connotations of objects such as Brutus's dagger, Caesar's will, Caesar's mantle, and Caesar's body with its wounds, students can examine the emotional associations each speaker conjures.

Maguire notes, "The introduction of Caesar's will illustrates another no-fail technique in public speaking, one which has nothing to do with classical rhetoric and therefore no technical term to define it: the use of props" (117). Besides Caesar's will, what else about the setting does Antony harness that Brutus ignores? They can view various film versions to see how directors have actors use the set. Ask students to draw modern parallels by thinking about the settings that various politicians use in our culture when making key speeches. How do the elements of setting (background and props near the speakers) affect our perception of the speech?

Handout 3.1, Rhetorical Techniques

Anaphora: Repetition of a word or phrase as the beginning of successive clauses.

- "... **we shall fight** on the beaches, **we shall fight** on the landing grounds, **we shall fight** in the fields and in the streets, **we shall fight** in the hills. **We shall** never surrender." (Winston Churchill)

- "**I have a dream** that one day even the state of Mississippi, a state, sweltering with the heat of injustice, sweltering with the heat of oppression, will be transformed into an oasis of freedom and justice. **I have a dream** that my four little children will one day live in a nation where they will not be judged by the color of their skin but by the content of their character. **I have a dream** today." (Dr. Martin Luther King)

Antithesis: The pairing of opposite or contrasting statements.

- "To be or not to be" (Hamlet) or "Ask not what your country can do for you—ask what you can do for your country" (John F. Kennedy)

- "It was the best of times, it was the worst of times, it was the age of wisdom, it was the age of foolishness . . ." (Charles Dickens, *A Tale of Two Cities*)

Epanalepsis: Words repeated at the beginning and the end of phrases, clauses, and sentences.

- A commercial for an anti-itch cream may say, "**Got** an itch? What an itch you've **got**!"

- "**Be** all that you can **be**." (Advertising slogan of the U.S. Army)

- "**Mankind** must put an end to war—or war will put an end to **mankind**." (John F. Kennedy, speech at the United Nations, 1961)

Hyberbaton: An inversion or reordering of words that should be in sequence.

- "Sorry I be but go you must." (Yoda in *Star Wars*)

- "Object there was none. Passion there was none." (Edgar Allan Poe, *The Tell-Tale Heart*)

Metaphor: A comparison of unrelated subjects to find a similarity; an equation of two unlike things to draw a comparison.

- "Language is a road map of a culture. It tells you where its people come from and where they are going." (Rita Mae Brown)

- "Life's but a walking shadow; a poor player, / That struts and frets his hour upon the stage." (Shakespeare, *Macbeth*)

---

continued on next page

Metonymy: Substitution of a word for a larger person, place, thing, or idea; use of a word that is associated with the original word.

- "The White House called for a meeting on economic policy today." ("The White House" substitutes for, "The President and his or her staff.")

- "By the sweat of my brow . . ." in which "sweat" is a substitute representing "hard work."

- "Houston, we have a problem." (Houston substitutes for NASA Mission Control.)

Paralepsis: The mention of something to emphasize its lack of importance, all the while emphasizing its importance.

- "Who said she was a jerk and couldn't be trusted? I would never say that."

- "I will not even mention the fact that you betrayed us . . ." (Cicero)

- "Too often has the scene in the dentist's waiting-room been described for me to try to do it again here. They are all alike. The antiseptic smell, the ominous hum from the operating-rooms, the ancient *Digests*, and the silent, sullen group of waiting patients . . ." Robert Benchley

---

Personification: A comparison in which an object or inanimate item is given human qualities or abilities.

> Because I could not stop for Death—
> He kindly stopped for me—
> The Carriage held but just Ourselves—
> And Immortality.
> —Emily Dickinson, "Because I Could Not Stop for Death"

Rhetorical question: A question that assumes the answer is known, asked for dramatic effect in order to make a claim.

- Is the sky blue?

- Why me?

- "How many roads must a man walk down/Before you call him a man?" (Bob Dylan)

Synecdoche: A substitution of the whole for the part or the part for the whole.

- "Hungry mouths to feed," in which "mouths" represents people.

continued on next page

- "Put a roof over our heads," in which "roof" stands for "house."

Tapinosis: Repeated language used to demean or disgrace someone or something.

- "Listen up, maggots. **You** are not special. **You** are not a beautiful or unique snowflake. **You're** the same decaying organic matter as everything else." (Tyler Durden in the film *Fight Club*, 1999)

Rhetorical Techniques, Answer Key

Anaphora
Brutus:

- "Who is here so base that would be a bondman? If any, speak, for him have I offended. Who is here so rude . . ."
- "As he was fortunate . . . as he was valiant . . . as he was ambitious . . ."

Antithesis

- *Brutus:* "Not that I lov'd Caesar less, but that I lov'd Rome more."
- *Antony:* "I come to bury Caesar, not to praise him."

Epanalepsis

- *Brutus:* ". . . hear me for my cause, and be silent, that you may hear. Believe me for mine honor, and have respect to mine honor, that you may believe."

Hyberbaton

- *Antony:* ". . . and grievously hath Caesar answer'd it."
- *Brutus:* "Then none have I offended."

Metaphor

- *Antony:* ". . . sweet Caesar's wounds, poor, poor, dumb mouths . . ." (also personification)

Metonymy
Antony:

- ". . . lend me your ears."
- "My heart is in the coffin there with Caesar."
- "But yesterday the word of Caesar might / Have stood against the world . . ." (also personification)

Paralepsis

- *Antony:* "Let but the commons hear this testament—/ Which, pardon me, I do not mean to read—"

Personification

- *Brutus:* ". . . awake your senses that you may be the better judge."

continued on next page

- *Antony:* "O judgment, thou art fled to brutish beasts . . ."
- *Antony:* ". . . Our Caesar's vesture wounded?"

Rhetorical Question
Brutus:

- "Had you rather Caesar were living . . . ?"
- "Who is here so base that would be a bondman?"
- "Who is here so rude that would not be a Roman?"
- "Who is here so vile that will not love his country?"
- ". . . a place in the commonwealth, as which of you shall not?"

Antony:

- "Did this in Caesar seem ambitious?"
- "Was this ambition?"
- "What cause withholds you then to mourn for him?"
- "For if you should, O, what would come of it?"
- "Kind souls, what weep you when you but behold / Our Caesar's vesture wounded?"

Synecdoche
Antony:

- ". . . if I were dispos'd to stir / Your hearts and minds to mutiny and rage . . ."

Tapinosis
Antony:

- "And Brutus is an honourable man." Honourable is repeated several times.
- ". . . Brutus says he was ambitious . . ." Ambitious is repeated several times.

Teaching Julius Caesar: *A Differentiated Approach* © 2010 Lyn Fairchild Hawks.

Suggested Passages for CRs and Essential Questions

If you choose some of these suggested passages to create CRs, encourage students to identify new big ideas they see in the text. Listed with each CR passage are more big ideas to explore as well as motifs worthy of tracking.

Remember to keep CRs to a brief amount of text, while increasing the number of lines with each act. Emphasize translation, annotation, and critical thinking questions.

For some passages, you will see models of play-related questions connected to big ideas and relevance questions. Play-related questions help a student investigate a character action or a plot event, staying within the framework of the play. Relevance questions tap into global, thematic connections that help students see how the play matters to us as individuals and as a society.

Together, these two types of questions create essential questions, the investigative queries that help students connect *Julius Caesar* to their lives and universal concerns. See page 169, Socratic Questions for Discussion and Writing, for the overarching questions that can drive unit study. Certain passages offer blanks for you to brainstorm questions to probe the play and the big idea.

- **Caesar, senators, scene 1 (OT/ADV):** "Are we all ready?" to "And constant do remain to keep him so." (Big ideas: appearance, arrogance, conspiracy, constancy, deception, flattery, honesty, manipulation, persuasion, power, pride, revenge. New big ideas: motifs: blood, dogs, stars.) EQ: *How constant is Caesar? How honest are the conspirators? What do these characterizations mean for Rome?*

> When students find new big ideas, remind them to make connections with other big ideas to form word families. Arrogance and pride can be connected to flattery, manipulation, and power. Help students see nuances and hone precision for writing topic sentences and thesis statements later.

- **Caesar, senators, scene 1 (ELL/NOV):** "Et tu, Brute?" to "... But we the doers." (Big ideas: ambition, chaos, conspiracy, cowardice, deception, fear, frailty, free will, honesty, honor, idealism.) EQs: *What is the first consequence of the conspirators' choices? How might that consequence be symbolic of what is to come? What values* *does Brutus declare for the new republic? How will this new order of government be conducted? Are the conspirators on the side of right, or does their deed seem to signify they are allied with something else?*

- **Cassius, Brutus, Casca, Decius, scene 1 (NOV/OT):** "Where is Antony?" to "With the most boldest and best hearts of Rome." (Big ideas: chaos, courage, fear, fate, free will, glory, history, honor, leadership, loyalty, patriotism. Motifs: acting, daggers/swords, blood.) EQs: *How do the conspirators perceive their act, in light of history? How does history, from our modern point of view, perceive their act?*

- **Brutus, Servant, Cassius, scene 1 (NOV/OT):** "Soft, who comes here?" to "Falls shrewdly to the purpose." (Big ideas: courage, fear, honor, idealism, love, loyalty, persuasion, realism.) EQs: *What are the differences in Brutus's and Cassius's approaches to Antony? Which approach is best for Brutus? For Cassius? For Rome?*

- **Antony, Brutus, Cassius, scene 1 (NOV/OT):** "O mighty Caesar!" to "Have thus proceeded." (Big ideas: glory, honor, love, loyalty, patience, patriotism, persuasion, pity, power. Motifs: blood, fire, swords.) EQs: _____

    _____

- **Antony, Cassius, Brutus, scene 1 (ADV):** "I doubt not of your wisdom" to "I know not what may fall, I like it not." (Big ideas: courage, flattery, grief, honesty, idealism, manipulation, nature, realism, savagery. Motifs: hands, blood, ghosts, deer, eyes/sight.) EQs: _____

    _____

- **Antony, Servant, scene 1 (OT/ADV):** "O, pardon me, thou ..." to "Lend me your hand." (Big ideas: courage, fate, ghosts, revenge. Motifs: curse, hands, dogs.) EQs: _____

    _____

My Ideas for Excerpts for CRs, from Scenes 2 and 3

Examine scenes 2 and 3 to find excerpts for students to analyze in CRs.

Scene _____ Lines _____ Readiness level: _____
Big ideas: _____
Motifs: _____
EQs: _____

Scene _____ Lines _____ Readiness level: _____
Big ideas: _____
Motifs: _____
EQs: _____

Scene _____ Lines _____ Readiness level: _____
Big ideas: _____
Motifs: _____
EQs: _____

Sample Performance Lesson: The Actor's Workshop: Scenelet Doubling and Analysis

Shakespeare challenges us to see characters in new lights and shadows by doubling scenes and moments. We see Cassius and Brutus in private conversation, followed by Caesar and Antony in private conversation; we see Portia pleading with Brutus, followed by Calpurnia pleading with Caesar. We can note similarities and contrasts to develop a greater understanding of Shakespeare's characters. Along with literary analysis, students can play the roles of actors and directors striving to make sense of a scene before performance. In this lesson, students practice scenelets in TR or MR groups and present them to other MR groups where they draw conclusions about characterization.

Quick Start to a Performance Lesson (90 minutes)

1. Explain to students the importance of (a) workshopping a scene to test out lines, abilities, and actor relationships and (b) comparing scenes to see how Shakespeare wrestles with big ideas such as love, loyalty, trust, and deception.

2. Review with students the analysis questions that will (a) drive their group's decisions about how to perform the scene and then (b) drive the two-group meeting where they perform for one another. Select questions your students most need to explore at this point, and scaffold the questions into readiness levels.

   a. What are characters' motives? How do actions, gestures, and speech demonstrate motives—and a big idea?

   b. What is the conflict in this scene? How does it demonstrate a big idea?

   c. How can costumes and props demonstrate big ideas?

   d. How can we create balance of movement on stage? How can actors fully use the space (heights to show power and other big ideas)?

   e. How does language delivery create pace, momentum, and show big ideas?

   f. How can character emotions/gestures/movement repre-sent big ideas and lead the audience to draw conclusions, or essential understandings? How can the director make sure that the acting works together to express the big idea(s)?

3. Review the Presentation Rubric (page 137) and ask if there are any questions.

4. Review group roles with students (you can limit to three roles or divide into more specific tasks): director/actor, who leads discussion, builds consensus about how to perform the scene, and also performs; actors/stage managers, who act the scene while suggesting blocking, props, costumes, and scenery; and analyst, who poses analysis questions for discussion before the scene is practiced and also later during the two-group meeting. Not everyone must act, but all group members should contribute to scene practice, performance, and analysis.

5. Break the class into student- or teacher-selected small groups of triads or quads. Assign scenelets. Circulate to ensure groups analyze first, and then begin a collaborative practice.

If you allow student-selected groups, encourage choice on the basis of scene challenge and interests. Review the levels of challenge, explaining to students why a scene is A or B level. Also ask students to sign up on a public Help Wanted ad—roles they want to perform such as director, actor, set designer, costume designer, props manager, soundtrack coordinator, etc. Students can look here before forming groups to ensure a balance of talents. If you select the MR groups, place ADV actors with low reading skills with ADV readers with low acting skills. As you circulate, remind students of "ABC," and compliment groups that support these goals: A = All Participate; B = Build on Everyone's Strengths; and C = Create Consensus.

---

6. Ask groups to join together for the two-group meeting (example: Groups 1.a and 1.b meet to perform and compare scenes— see Suggested Scenelets on page 160). These two groups will now perform their scenes, then discuss these doubling analysis questions:

   a. How are character motives similar in both scenes? How are they different?

   b. How is the conflict both similar and different?

   c. How are the big ideas both similar and different?

   d. What essential questions do these scenes raise? What essential understandings, or themes, derive from these questions? Are these scenes making the same or different statements? (Note: This is a good time to help students, especially ELL/NOV, convert the abstract nouns of big ideas to phrases and complete sentences. Discussion will provide a safe space to test out their "thesis theories." ADV students can start asking tough essential questions that lead to essential understandings about character, plot, and other elements of the play—which will lead to stronger thesis statements.)

7. Bring groups together for a WCA discussion to report results of these discussions.

If students need more guidance in preparing a scene, see the sample lesson offered in Act 3 of *Teaching* Romeo and Juliet: *A Differentiated Approach*. Its template for student notes and other management tips apply to this activity. You can also ask students to select only a few analysis questions. Once groups choose big ideas to represent, a note-taking activity can focus on scene planning: by writing the big ideas in the middle of a sheet of paper, students can web out how motives/gestures/actions, use of space, pace, and delivery can represent these ideas and then answer these scene-planning questions as they relate to that big idea.

Suggested Scenelets

Act, scene, lines	Characters	Big ideas	Suggested readiness level
Group 1.a: act 1, scene 2: Caesar: "Antonio" to "tell me truly what thou think'st of him."	Antony, Caesar	TRUST, AMBITION, LOYALTY, FEAR, ENVY, LEADERSHIP, REALISM	A (ELL/NOV)
Group 1.b: act 1, scene 2: Brutus: "Another general shout!" to Cassius: "encompass'd but one man?"	Brutus, Cassius	TRUST, ENVY, FATE, AMBITION, GLORY, FREE WILL, CONSPIRACY, LEADERSHIP	B (OT/ADV)
Group 2.a: act 1, scene 2: Brutus: "That you do love me . . ." to Cassius: "much show of fire from Brutus" and Cassius's soliloquy: "Well, Brutus, thou art noble . . . or worse days endure."	Brutus, Cassius	CONSTANCY, MANIPULATION, HONOR, LOVE, PERSUASION, AMBITION	A (ELL/NOV)
Group 2.b: act 3, scene 1: Caesar: "I must prevent thee . . ." to ". . . and constant do remain to keep him so."	Caesar, Metellus, Brutus, Cassius	CONSTANCY, MANIPULATION, AMBITION	B (OT/ADV)

Notes

- These are suggested big ideas but not complete lists of options.

- Group 1.a and 1.b: Possible themes to explore in these paired scenes: Caesar is wise to Cassius's envy, which shows Caesar's leadership abilities, realism, and insight into men's hearts. Cassius is so consumed with envy and ambition that his rant displays not love or loyalty to Rome, but rather, resentment that one should rise above him. His argument lacks hard facts and uses emotional appeals. The question of friendship arises: does the relationship between Caesar and Antony show greater trust and loyalty than that of Cassius and Brutus? Another question to explore is one of fate and free will: can awareness of other men's flaws protect a leader, or do others' ambitions (such as the conspirators) consign Caesar to be a pawn of fate?

- For Groups 2.a and 2.b: Possible themes to explore in these paired scenes: the question of who is most constant and steadfast. Cassius claims that Brutus can be manipulated; Caesar claims he cannot be swayed because he is eternally constant. These questions lead to questions of who may make a better leader of Rome. Keep in mind that both men are subject to persuasion by their wives.

Suggested Scenelets, continued

Act, scene, lines	Characters	Big ideas	Suggested readiness level
Group 3.a: act 2, scene 1: Portia: "Is Brutus sick?" to Brutus: ". . . worthy of this noble wife!"	Portia, Brutus	LOVE, LOYALTY, TRUST, HONESTY, COURAGE	B (OT/ADV)
Group 3.b: act 2, scene 2: Calpurnia: "What mean you, Caesar . . ." to Caesar: "Will come when it will come."	Caesar, Calpurnia	LOVE, TRUST, LOYALTY, FATE, COURAGE, COWARDICE	B (OT/ADV)
Group 4.a: act 3, scene 2: Brutus: "I have done no more . . ." to "till Antony have spoke."	Brutus and First, Second, Third, and Fourth Plebeians	GLORY, HONOR, LOVE, PATRIOTISM, LOYALTY, PERSUASION, CHAOS, LEADERSHIP	A (ELL/NOV)
Group 4.b: act 3, scene 2: Fourth Plebeian	Antony and Fourth, Second, and Third Plebeians	MANIPULATION, PERSUASION, LOVE, LOYALTY, CHAOS, LEADERSHIP	A (ELL/NOV)

Notes

- These are suggested big ideas but not complete lists of options.

- For Groups 3.a. and 3.b: Possible themes to explore in these paired scenes: the loyalty, trust, and love that these protagonists have with their wives and how each woman is greatly concerned, if not prescient, about the danger her husband is in. By giving us a window into these men's private lives, Shakespeare shows us that their most intimate relationships are built on integrity and closeness, and also touched by fear. We also see that the work of flatterers and conspirators overshadows the bond that they have with their wives. These men can be persuaded by love, which shows that they have motives of integrity. Their tendency to be persuaded (or lack of constancy) leads to questions of how easily manipulated both men might be, how frail, and how fit to lead.

- For Groups 4.a and 4.b: Possible themes to explore in these paired scenes: each man's ability to lead and manage the potential chaos that could be started by angry citizens; each man's ability to be a politician, if a politician is defined by arts of persuasion and acting. What are they each persuading the people to do, and why? To what is each man most loyal? Has each man done the right thing that a good leader should do?

Suggestions for Performance and Cinematic Analysis Lesson

In act 3, scene 3, a mob of Roman citizens mistakes Cinna the Poet for Cinna the Conspirator. The scene is both black comedy and tragedy and a precursor to the violence that grips the final acts of the play. This scene raises essential questions for students to explore:

- How does chaos erupt in a community? What leads to mob behavior?

- Who is to blame for what occurs in this scene?

- What word families can we build with chaos? (Fear, revenge, trust, loyalty, and love are some big ideas that can be connected as causes).

Here are tips for designing a performance and cinematic analysis activity. You can assign the skits and research prompts as homework or classwork for a prelude to the group work activity.

Understanding Chaos and Mob Rule: Skits and Research

- Ask students to write or improvise skits about causes of chaos in modern life. Give them recognizable settings—a public park, a campus, a DMV, a store, a sports event, etc. Ask them to identify character motives (motive matchsticks) that could spark conflict and chaos in these places.

- Ask students to search current events articles for historical incidents in the last year that show chaos. Ask them to look at politics, sports, economics, the arts, race and class relations, and other aspects of our culture and society to identify motives and conflict.

- They can perform scenes or report current events in a WCA. Ask students to compare their invented or real scenarios to act 3, scene 3, using the previous questions.

Understanding Chaos and Mob Rule: Cinematic Analysis

Note to students that the 1953 and 1970 film versions of *Julius Caesar* omit act 3, scene 3. Therefore, it is a creative opportunity for students to break new ground cinematically. Their task is to construct a cinematic storyboard or directorial freeze frame showing how they would render this scene on film. They might consider everything from line selection, casting, acting, camera angles, blocking/staging, costumes, soundtrack, and acting in order to express the big ideas (such as chaos and revenge) in this scene.

- Materials needed: copies of the scene that students can mark up; box of props; and posterboard, art paper, or electronic slide shows/Web design software for groups who want to storyboard.

- Review Handout 3.2, *Julius Caesar* on Film, (page 165), which defines elements of a film's "cinematic texture." Explain how these elements are critical to a film version of a Shakespeare play, illustrating the director's interpretation of the script. Explain that Shakespeare's text is often cut and even rewritten. You can review camera angle terms by asking a student to pose as a cameraperson and take the position from which the shots will be made; by asking students to sketch out shots or angles; or by asking them to use a lightweight picture frame to "frame" people in the room as if captured in a shot. Students can also share examples of famous shots or angles from films.

For a fun introduction to the importance of sound effects, play the NPR radio podcasts listed in Works Cited (page 217) about the creative work of foley artists (sound effects) and costume designers.

- Explain that their task in groups is not just to implement technique while filming but to also present an overarching purpose, or understanding, of the text. You're not looking just for style but substance: the big ideas, essential questions, and essential understandings this scene raises. Post the rubric that you design for this activity.

- Ask students to meet in MR interest groups to read the scene aloud, practice staging, and make decisions to draw or perform elements, such as camera angles, acting, and staging. They are welcome to include other elements.

If students need practice connecting lines and cinematic technique to big ideas, try one or more of the following activities: (a) Discuss how Cinna's opening line, "I dreamt tonight that I did feast with Caesar" could be acted / staged / angled to communicate fear or chaos. Example: a shot of Cinna hurrying through the streets, with fast camera movement and close-ups of his furrowed brow to show fear, and the sound track could capture his heaving breaths. (b) View the 1950 version of Antony's speech to the citizens (act 3, scene 2), particularly the last few lines where we get a close-up of Antony's smirking face to show us he intended to rile the crowd to mutiny, with the scene of the rioters behind him. Explain how a big idea of manipulation appears here through directorial and actor choices for staging, angle, and facial expression.

- Students will then present either their
  - ◆ storyboard (shot by shot in poster or electronic form, matched with lines as captions) or
  - ◆ freeze frame (the scene acted out, with one student playing "cameraperson" and the other playing director, interrupting action to narrate the angles and staging that would occur during filming).
  - ◆ Groups are welcome to create a soundtrack for the scene. Sound track can be more than music and should include an array of auditory effects.
- Lead students in giving feedback on the creativity of groups' choices and the integration of big ideas via cinematic technique. Students should be encouraged to pose essential questions and state tentative essential understandings.

Handout 3.2, *Julius Caesar* on Film

Choices toward Cinematic Texture

Casting: Decisions about who will act various roles.

Costume design: Wardrobe and accessories, determined by setting, time period, and mood.

Scenery and props: Elements establishing setting and space, determined by time period, action, and mood.

Sound track: Music selected to create mood and setting.

Cinematic shots/camera angles: The movement in the shot, the length of the shot, and the angle of the screen image. A *cut* is a shift between two different camera shots.

Camera Work: Movement, Angle, and Length

Movement: (1) a series of cuts that go from one shot to the next or (2) moving the camera with the action—a slower option because the amount of visual information on the screen decreases in relation to time, as compared to a series of quick cuts. Some methods of camera movement include (a) **zoom lens shot:** a shot that moves the viewer in or out of a scene quickly without the camera having to move while filming, often giving a distorted sense of the people or objects on screen; (b) **aerial shots:** taken from a helicopter, often used as "establishing shots" at the film's beginning, allowing the camera to move fluidly about the landscape; (c) **handheld shots:** the camera is attached with a harness to the camera operator, allowing the operator to move in and out of shots speedily; provides a bumpy visual experience for the viewer and thus the impression of realism (versus a dolly shot); (d) **tilts:** vertical camera movement through the scene; (e) **pans:** horizontal camera movement through the scene.

Angle: The placement of the camera in relation to the subject being photographed. The angle at which the subject is recorded provides hints about the importance of what shows on screen.

Oblique/canted angle: Tilted, nonhorizontal angle used in point-of-view shots to allow the viewer to closely experience the fear, unsteadiness, or unease of a character.

Eye level: Angle where the viewer observes the scene as if at eye level with the actors.

Low angle: Angle low to the ground and tilted up so the object or actor in the frame appears larger than it or he or she is and perhaps quite intimidating.

High angle: Version of the bird's-eye view, less severe with the camera less elevated.

Bird's-eye view: Angle where the viewer looks straight down on the scene from overhead. Objects can be made unrecognizable or people, small and insignificant.

continued on next page

Length of shot (framing of the shot): Expanse of the shot, determined by what people, objects, and landscape appear in the camera's frame.

Close-up shot: Shot that focuses the viewer's eye on a face, an object, or a landscape detail, magnifying it across the screen, with the goal to express importance of whatever is in the frame. With a character, the shot suggests that we are entering the mind of the character.

Point-of-view shot: Shot from the point of view of a character, so the viewer experiences the action from the perspective of this character interacting with other characters.

Over-the-shoulder shot: Medium shot where the camera looks over the shoulder of one character during a conversation so that viewers focus on one character at a time.

Medium shot: A shot that shows interaction between characters by framing them from the chest up. Often used for dialogue scenes, the shot normally contains two to three people.

Long shot: Shot showing action and characters life-size with their full bodies on screen.

Extreme long shot: "Establishing shot," letting viewers know where the action occurs; an exterior shot from far away (see **bird's-eye view**).

Sample Mini-Lesson: Iambic Pentameter: Five Stresses Are All You've Got

Materials needed: Antony's line posted: "I speak not to disprove what Brutus spoke, / But here I am to speak what I do know."

Explain: Shakespeare's lines usually have about ten beats, or syllables, per line. We care about rhythm for several reasons: (1) good rhythm leads to good speaking; (2) rhythm places beats on certain words, which gives us a clue as to what is important to a character or the plot; and (3) a ten-syllable rhythm per line is a rule showing how creative Shakespeare could be within constraints.

Direct: With a partner, find a passage in act 3, scene 2, of four to six lines; count the number of syllables per line. How often in each of the lines do you count ten syllables?

Explain: Sometimes Shakespeare goes over or under ten beats, but never by many. When he does, pay close attention. Imagine having a syllable limit for every sentence you write!

In director Baz Luhrmann's film of *Romeo and Juliet*, a modern newscaster delivers the lines of the prologue. Why? Listen to the number of words a person can say before taking a breath: one to two sentences, in about ten beats, or iambic pentameter.

Direct: Take the role of newscaster or speechmaker. Write a two- to three-sentence introduction to one of the following topics, using ten syllables per line:

- A breaking news report
- A speech accepting an award you hope to win someday
- Sports commentary during a high-stakes athletic contest

News Report Example
"Today in quaint and quiet Westin Town /
police came when a 911 call said /
a murder had occurred at 1 Park Lane."
Speech Example
"Good evening, judges, fans, family, and friends; /
I am honored to receive this award."
Sports Report Example
"State now faces Tech. A bitter rival /
Since '68, Tech hopes to end State's reign."

Direct: Was it easy or hard to use ten beats per line? Why or why not? Let's discuss.

Explain: Shakespeare used this rhythm, called unrhymed *iambic pentameter*, or *blank verse*. An *iamb* is a two-beat, or two-syllable, section of a line. In an iamb, the first beat is unstressed while the second beat is stressed. An iamb is like the human heartbeat: Thud-THUD.

Direct: Read aloud to your partner the sentences you wrote, slowly and carefully, while your partner uses a pencil, hands, or feet to tap, clap, or stomp out the rhythm. If the words or syllables that are stressed aren't that important, what words or phrases can you change? Note that in example #3, stresses fall on key words such as "hopes," "end," and "reign."

Explain: *Pentameter*: *Penta* means "five" (think pentagon, five sides), and *meter* means "rhythm," or the number of beats per line. Poets also call the iamb a metric foot, because back in the days of the ancient Greek choruses, actors in the chorus would walk one step, or foot, for each syllable until they came to the end of a line. Then they turned to walk back across the stage.

Explain: When you scan a line, mark the iambic pentameter like this (here, during Brutus's funeral speech in act 3, scene 2):

Do gráce to Cáesar's córpse, and gráce his spéech

Direct: Note how key words such as "grace," "corpse," and "speech" receive the emphasis. Why is this important?

Explain:

- Caesar's **corpse** is the subject—what should be done with it—so that word gets emphasis.

- Brutus's values emerge via **"grace"**: he is perceived as a man of honor, so he will not see Caesar's body defiled by the mob, and he believes the people should give Antony respect.

- There is also irony in the repetition of **grace**. The murder of Caesar has been anything but graceful, so is Brutus really true to his values? Grace also has the connotation of God's sanctification and redemption of humans despite their sin. Can there be grace for the sin of killing Caesar, especially for a man with the symbolic initials J.C.? An essential question for us to ponder.

- Finally, **speech** is very important in this play: who speaks best wins the hearts and minds of the people.

Write "corpse" and "grace" for students and show through webbing the connotations listed here, how big ideas, and essential questions can be derived from close analysis. **Direct:** With your partner, scan the following line from Antony's funeral speech. Put a slash mark above the syllables where stresses fall in each iamb.

"I spéak not tó dispróve what Brútus spóke, /
But hére I ám to spéak what Í do knów."

Direct: Which words or syllables are stressed? Which are key words that connect to a big idea?

Explain: See how speech is again stressed through the use of "speak" and "spoke"? Note also how the big ideas of persuasion and manipulation appear through words such as *disprove*.

Direct: With a partner or a group of three, practice the scene I give you by reading it aloud. Prepare to present to the class in a rhythmic way using claps, stomps, or some other percussion that shows us iambic pentameter at work. Then explain to the class how key words lead to big ideas. Together we will try to draw essential questions or understandings from the big ideas you pinpoint. This is practice for commentary you will soon be crafting in your essays. (Give each group an excerpt of six to ten lines to present.)

Socratic Questions for Discussion and Writing

All activities, assignments, and assessments should be driven by essential questions: the whys, the what ifs, and the shoulds. Essential questions are synonymous with Socratic questions—the analysis, evaluation, and synthesis questions for discussion and essay topics that all students can be coached to answer. Up until now, CRs and WCA discussions have modeled this critical thinking. Act 3 is a great time to hand students the reins in both discussion and writing.

Philosophy and Ground Rules for Discussion

Socratic seminars challenge students to explore important issues; to communicate clearly, substantively, and respectfully; and to deepen understanding of the text. The teacher's role is to keep questioning alive; to encourage students to use the text for evidence, to encourage thoughtful commentary on evidence, to provide feedback on discussion progress; to nurture positive behaviors; and to delegate discussion facilitation to students, eventually playing observer rather than catalyst. For a Socratic discussion to be a success, students must own the conversation.

Establish and review the ground rules using Handout 3.3, Socratic Seminar Evaluation Rubric (page 178), before the first discussion (thirty minutes or longer).

> If this is the first unit where you are attempting Socratic discussion, expect discussion to be halting, tentative, or even chaotic until students understand routines. A safe way to begin introducing rules and ensuring a successful start is to spend one full class period reviewing the rubric and using a film clip as the "text" for analysis. Pose the question, "Is Antony a responsible leader? What does the film evidence show?" and then watch a portion of his act 3, scene 2 speech. Provide positive feedback for students who live up to the rubric. As you begin your first discussion, keep in mind only two essential goals: establish clear, firm ground rules and pose rigorous questions. Other criteria on the rubric can be addressed and practiced in later discussions.

Before a discussion, ask students to prepare notes using Handout 3.4, Socratic Seminar Notes (page 179). In class, have students sit in a circle or U shape, and if there are observers, in an outer ring. Students should come prepared with both notes and texts.

You can assign roles such as question leader (the person who ensures ample time for discussion of each question and invites new questions) and evidence checker (the person who asks that speakers defend their claims with quotations, paraphrases, or reasons). Depending on personality types and learning styles, some students prefer speaking in generalizations, while others prefer speaking in specifics. Whatever their preference, all must learn to quote or paraphrase the text to defend an argument, and all must eventually extrapolate topical subgroups and generalizations (the big ideas and essential understandings) from the specifics. Good speakers and writers move fluidly between the concrete and the abstract.

Handout 3.3, Socratic Seminar Evaluation Rubric, (page 178) provides criteria for evaluating student performance and should be used by both you and students. Handout 3.4, Socratic Seminar Notes (page 179) students can use for record-keeping and gather evidence for later work on essay prompts and projects.

Possible Seminar Formats

- *TR differentiation*: NOV, OT, and ADV groups can discuss separately in TR groups of seven to ten students, meaning you will be supervising three or more discussion groups simultaneously.

Or, TR groups can be matched up to observe and evaluate each other (fish bowl style) and then switch halfway through class or during the next class session. Assign different questions to each group to create the richest discussion later when the class regroups. Note that relevance questions (see page 172) can be more ELL/NOV friendly in the first times you lead discussions, since they are less dependent on strong reading comprehension. Also consider "chunking" discussion into 25-minute experiences until students grow more comfortable with the guidelines.

- *MR differentiation*: Make two discussion groups of ten to fifteen each: one, an ELL/NOV/OT mix and the other, an OT/ADV mix. Or, make each group completely heterogeneous. Have each group discuss different questions while the other group assesses using the rubric. This fish bowl observation format allows students to model for one another and practice compliments and constructive criticism. You might have a group with the strongest speakers go first and thus model for the other group.

- *WCA*: Have all students seminar together. The most heterogeneous mix allows the richest variety of perspectives, in which students with practical wisdom might educate those with more sheltered perspectives and verbal-linguistic students can model a love of close reading, debate, and language for less avid readers. This format can be more difficult to manage if you have a particularly large class and extreme ranges of readiness levels. Some students may be intimidated by ADV students' verbal prowess and be reluctant to appear intellectual. Rely heavily on relevance questions for initial WCA discussions while emphasizing two core skills: listening respectfully and offering evidence.

- A note about compacting and ADV students: Those who read ahead should be told not to give spoilers. These students can still benefit from intensive study of a particular act. Explain that untapped evidence can be found in the acts the class is now discussing, and that reading is not a rush to the finish but a slow walk with many stops to enjoy the view. ADV readers can practice the art of finding the more complex and obscure evidence, which requires higher-level analysis, such as commentary on connotation, iambic pentameter, and motif. Profoundly gifted students need individualized conferences or TR seminars to allow deeper exploration, so make arrangements for meetings with you or an appropriate mentor.

Consider the lesson flow at this point in the unit: do you need to teach a mini-lesson to ELL/NOV students who need help with translation or other concepts such as key words and topic sentences? If so, you can meet with those TR groups while other TR groups of OT/ADV students run discussions in groups of ten or less. This scenario is most ideal if the OT/ADV students know rules and roles and/or you have another instructor or adult volunteer. The next day, switch and offer mini-lessons in needed skills to OT/ADV while the other adult supervises the ELL/NOV discussion. Or, provide audio- or video-recording devices so you can review later.

Types of Socratic Questions

Play-related questions are "local" queries, targeting character, plot, and theme, whereas relevance questions are "global" queries exploring students' preconceived understandings and definitions, attitudes, and experiences as they relate to the big ideas and essential questions. Relevance questions demand evidence, too: appropriate personal anecdotes and real life examples, any statistics or facts students know offhand, as well as historical and current events. Use relevance questions as a launching pad for engaging discussion, and then move back into the text of the play. Or, begin with play-related questions and expand outward to draw parallels and contrasts with "real-world" events. Relevance questions can also serve as journal prompts throughout the unit, whereas play-related questions serve as essay prompts. The ADV essay question blends both play-related and relevance questions.

Personal anecdotes can enrich a Socratic discussion. An effective personal anecdote is one that is relevant to all listeners and is shared to connect more deeply with the text. For example, "I learned about honesty when I was six and lied to my parents. They took away my favorite games. I'll always remember that incident and now honesty is very important to me. I don't trust Cassius because he is not being honest with Brutus; he has a secret agenda to manipulate him." Some students will need gentle guidance away from stories that get too personal, and be sure to let students know others' private information is off limits.

AMBITION
Relevance Questions:

- What are signs a person has a lot of ambition—or too much ambition?
- How do we know when ambition is healthy rather than dangerous—and vice versa?
- What ambitions should our government leaders have? Why?
- When should people "know their place" and refrain from too much ambition?

Play-Related Questions:

- Is any character too ambitious, such as Caesar, Cassius, Brutus, or Antony?
- Do any characters lack a realistic perception of others' ambitions? Where? How? What are the consequences of these misperceptions?

CONSTANCY
Relevance Questions:

- How do we define constancy? (The dictionary says constancy is the quality of being unchanging, firm, and faithful, in terms of love or loyalty. It also has connotations of regularity, invariability, and uniformity.)
- Where in our society do we most value constancy? In what ways?

Play-Related Questions:

- Caesar claims he is "constant as the Northern star" (3, 1). How accurate is his self-assessment? Is he impervious to flattery and persuasion?
- What form does Portia's "constancy" take? Calpurnia's? Do you approve of their devotion? Why or why not?
- How constant is Brutus?
- Which characters seem to be the opposite of constant? Why?

FATE and FREE WILL
Relevance Questions:

- Does fate exist? How do we define it?
- How much free will do we have?

Play-Related Questions:

- Caesar appears to accept his fate, while Cassius declares he will fight his circumstances. Whom are you inclined to believe at this stage of the play?
- Where do other characters seem to line up in terms of belief in fate versus free will?

LEADERSHIP
Relevance Questions:

- What is the difference between leadership and tyranny?
- Can leadership be shared, or is it always better to have one strong leader?
- Should leaders appeal to the hearts or the minds of the people?
- Does the average citizen want a leader or a tyrant?

Play-Related Questions:

- Is Caesar a good leader or a tyrant, as some of the conspirators claim?
- What type of leader is Brutus? Cassius? Antony? Octavius?
- How do Brutus and Cassius share leadership? Antony and Octavius?
- What type of leader do the Roman citizens value?
- How do leaders such as Caesar, Brutus, Cassius, and Antony appeal to the Romans—through their hearts or minds, or both?

FRAILTY
Relevance Questions:

- How frail is a leader allowed to be? In what ways?
- If a leader has a frailty, what is the best way to cope with that weakness?

Play-Related Questions:

- Is Caesar too frail to lead?
- What frailties do Brutus, Cassius, and Antony possess?
- How do Brutus and Cassius deal with one another's flaws?

GLORY
Relevance Questions:

- Should leaders receive special honors, or glories, for their accomplishments?
- Should literature show sympathies to all characters or glorify only those who are morally upright?
- Should people receive glory for killing someone?

Play-Related Questions:

- Is Caesar given too much glory, in life and in death?
- Whom does the play seem to glorify this far—if anyone?
- Is the murder of Caesar glorious, as Cassius indicates?

HEROISM
Relevance Questions:

- What makes a true hero?
- What makes an antihero?
- What makes a villain?

Play-Related Questions:

- Who is the hero of this play? The villain?
- Is there a character who is an antihero?
- How do the citizens of Rome define "hero"?

HONESTY
Relevance Question:

- Should you be completely honest with your spouse? With your friends? Your coworkers? Your boss?

Play-Related Questions:

- Which characters demonstrate the utmost honesty? The utmost dishonesty?
- Where do characters make a mistake in being too honest? In being less than honest?

HONOR
Relevance Questions:

- Is all fair in love and war?

- What is honorable behavior when it comes to friendship?
- What is honorable behavior in battle?
- Can suicide be considered honorable?

Play-Related Questions:

- Who behaves with the greatest honor in this play?
- Who violates the codes of honor? How?

IDEALISM
Relevance Questions:

- What idealism should leaders have?
- How idealistic may a leader be? Should a leader be more of a realist or an idealist?

Play-Related Questions:

- Does Brutus's idealism justify his actions?
- Should Brutus have followed Cassius's more realistic advice?

LOVE
Relevance Questions:

- Should you love your country more than family or friends?
- Should you ever show more love to friends than parents, family, or a partner?

Play-Related Questions:

- How would you describe the love between Brutus and Portia and the love between Calpurnia and Caesar?
- How would you describe the love between Cassius and Brutus?

LOYALTY
Relevance Questions:

- How do we show loyalty to our leaders or our country? For example, our President—what symbols of loyalty, both physical objects and rituals, demonstrate Americans' loyalty?
- How do we show loyalty to our friends?
- What is the ultimate test of loyalty to a friend? To leaders and country?

Play-Related Questions:

- What kind of loyalty is demanded of Romans by Rome?
- Who seems right now to be the most loyal friend to another person in the play?

MANIPULATION
Relevance Question:

- Can the average citizen be manipulated into believing someone is a hero?

Play-Related Questions:

- Which characters seem most manipulated in this play?
- Is there a character who is the consummate manipulator? What are the talents that make for success?

PATRIOTISM
Relevance Questions:

- What makes a true patriot?
- Does patriotism trump other values?

Play-Related Questions:

- How does Brutus's patriotism differ from Antony's?
- In what ways is patriotism both healthy and dangerous in certain characters?

POWER
Relevance Questions:

- How should people in power conduct themselves?
- What view of government power does Cicero, one of Caesar's contemporaries, present us with? Is it still relevant today? He wrote: "The budget should be balanced, the Treasury should be refilled, public debt should be reduced, the arrogance of officialdom should be tempered and controlled . . ." Marcus Tullius Cicero, 63 B.C. (qtd in Frederickson and Johnston)

Play-Related Questions:

- Does Caesar abuse his power?
- Do the senators abuse their power?
- Does Antony?
- Who uses power most wisely in the play?

Handout 3.3, Socratic Seminar Evaluation Rubric

Speaker_____ Observer_____

Ground Rules

- Respect all participants.
- Disagree with grace and courtesy.
- Participate selectively if you have a lot to say.
- Draw others into the discussion.
- Listen actively by watching the speaker and avoiding distractions.
- Build on others' points when you make yours.
- Speak once another speaker finishes.
- Support your claims with textual evidence.
- Evaluate your peers' performance with constructive criticism.

Behaviors	Advanced	On-Target	Novice
Shares the discussion rather than monopolizing or interrupting			
Listens to others by building on points previously made			
Raises new points; asks clarifying questions; and/or examines the logic of ideas			
Provides relevant supporting evidence from the text			
Respectfully disagrees			
Speaks loudly and clearly			
Provides relevant, appropriate real-life examples			

Comments:

Handout 3.4, Socratic Seminar Notes

Name _____ Period _____

Big Ideas: _____

Essential Question: _____

Essential Question	Play-Related Examples (text) act, scene, lines	Personal and Real-Life Examples

Teaching Julius Caesar: *A Differentiated Approach* © 2010 Lyn Fairchild Hawks.

Design Tips: Writing Assignments

In *Julius Caesar*, speaking is all about persuasion and is also a good model for the maxim that all writing is argument (Lunsford et al). During act 3, you can raise essay topics and ask students to think about where their interests lie. Handout 2.5, Topical Subgroups and Significant Particulars Chart (page 138) can be used throughout the rest of the unit as you steer students toward prompt choice and evidence gathering.

Since writing involves a wide range of skills and several stages of process, select those skills your students most need at this point in the school year. See Handout 3.6, Essay Rubric, and distill as necessary to emphasize skills that address core needs of all readiness levels. Return to "Core Competencies" on page xix for a reminder of what you can reasonably accomplish within this unit.

Lunsford et al. clarify that "the point of argument is to discover some version of the truth, using evidence and reasons. . . . The aim of persuasion is to change a point of view or to move others from conviction to action" (7). To prioritize and scaffold writing skills, make sure students can (a) see the specifics in the text as evidence and (b) extrapolate topical subgroups to build topic sentences. See Duke University Talent Identification Program's *The Writer's Journey, Volumes 1 and 2*, for detailed skill-building exercises for each phase of the writing process.

Make time to model the writing process, from prewriting to drafting to editing.

Prewriting involves:

- prompt selection,
- evidence-gathering (significant particulars), and
- generalization (topical subgroup development)

Drafting involves:

- mapping or outlining,
- topic sentence development from topical subgroups, and
- first draft writing.

Editing involves:

- peer review with constructive criticism,
- further revision (ideally, at least three drafts), and
- grammar and mechanics proofing.

What will happen at publication? Should you be the only audience? Consider the speaker's corner project on page 199 as a culmination of the writing process.

There is tremendous pressure on teachers to move swiftly to "cover" the standards and prep for tests. If you have your students practice core reading and writing skills throughout a Shakespeare unit, stopping to address what students don't know and can't do, you are also prepping students for standardized test skills, such as finding the topic sentence in a paragraph, identifying the main idea, and finding supporting details to prove the main idea. It's worth it to offer mini-lessons to TR groups to reinforce skills and spend less time reading the entire play. It's worth it to not charge ahead into a new book and instead "stay awhile" with Shakespeare and practice reading and writing skills that you will take to the next level in the next unit.

Students who can't translate or annotate can't select an essay prompt; students who don't understand significant particulars can't draw a conclusion; and students who can't draw conclusions can't build topic sentences and thesis statements. Therefore, keep your goals simple: (a) Do students understand this passage? (b) Can they find the details? (c) Can they draw a conclusion from these details? Even a student who hasn't read the whole play can write an effective analysis of a few pages of *Julius Caesar*.

For the ELL/NOV students who struggle with translation, adjust expectations for a Tier A essay prompt (See Handout 3.5, Essay Writing Prompts for *Julius Caesar*, A–C on page 184 for TR writing assignments). Asking students to focus on acts 1 through 3 while choosing significant particulars is a fair and reasonable requirement, narrowing the amount of text for them to consider, while emphasizing the importance of selecting the most significant details. A student pursuing a Tier C prompt should be challenged to see the play as a cohesive whole driven by big ideas, which is a high level of critical thinking, but he or she should not be held too accountable for not having mastered the semicolon or not truly understanding iambic pentameter, either. Again, see "Core Competencies" on page xix of the introduction for a reminder of what you and your students can reasonably accomplish within a unit.

Develop a plan of writing mini-lessons and writing practice balanced with close reading, performance, anchoring activities, and projects students can explore any day for the rest of the unit. A sample class block period integrating writing instruction might go as follows:

- In a very brief WCA, model an excellent set of topic sentences for a character analysis paragraph. Use a character studied earlier in the year, topic sentences from prior student papers, or ones that you develop about a popular movie or TV character. Provide models at the A, B, and C level.

- Have ELL/NOV students work on topic sentence development in a TR mini-lesson; while OT and ADV students work in MR partners to develop essay outlines.

- Close class with a scene performance, CR discussion, or cinematic analysis that asks students to create topic sentences about big ideas in the scene, passage, or film clip.

Or,

- In a very brief WCA, model excellent context and commentary for a character analysis paragraph—A, B, and C level.

- Teach OT/ADV students context and commentary development in a TR mini-lesson while ELL/NOV students work in TR pairs to find significant particulars for essay prompts.

- Provide class time to work on projects driven by essential questions and understandings.

For tips in setting up classroom routines and management, see Chapter 9, "How Do You Manage Differentiation?" in Heacox's *Differentiating Instruction in the Regular Classroom*.

See Handout 3.5, Essay Writing Prompts for *Julius Caesar*, A–C on page 184 for TR writing assignments. Note that options within each level increase in challenge. Option #1 will not require as many layers of skill and decision-making as Options #2 and #3. A-level prompts are also highly structured according to the five-paragraph structure, whereas levels B and C are less detailed and prescriptive. You may want to provide outlining handouts to assist ELL/NOV students in organizing their essays, using Handout 3.5 as a guide for structuring the elements of the outline.

If this is your first time offering TR essay prompts, be selective in your choices. Some classes might not need all these choices, and you may not wish to juggle them all. Some classes are so heterogeneous that levels A–C are required, while some need only a few choices from A and B. An honors course at the high school level can use the most advanced options from levels B and C. As you make your decisions, see Appendix B, Grading in a Differentiated Classroom on page 214.

How long should you give to the writing process? One solution: devote homework and class time to culling substantive significant particulars, development of precise topical subgroups, and development of clear and summative topic sentences. Then, offer a few class periods in which students write essays under your supervision. You can coach students while writing and also ensure that families, friends, and the Internet were not present at the creation. Revision can take place in one or more class periods, after you've given first-draft feedback, or at home for one night. You might also have time for a third draft after peer revision in class.

Handout 3.5, Essay Writing Prompts for *Julius Caesar* A

Directions: Choose a prompt. Complete the Topical Subgroups & Significant Particulars Chart.

Option #1, Character Analysis: Murderous Motives: A Report to the Police

Essay Question: What were the conspirators' motives?

Your Role: You are a police detective interviewing Cassius, Brutus, and Casca who are now in custody. (Let's pretend everyone made it out of this play alive.) As the crime scene investigator, you must reconstruct what caused the crime by examining conspirators' motives. You will share this objective report with your police chief, who will then provide your analysis to the prosecuting district attorney as evidence for pressing charges.

Your Task: Analyze one or more characters to determine motive(s) that led to the crime.

Audience: Chief of Police and District Attorney

Essay Structure:

- Paragraph 1, YOUR THESIS: Identify one or more characters and their motives that led to Caesar's murder. (Will you study Cassius, Brutus, and Casca, or two characters, or one? If you choose all three, choose one motive for each man. If you choose one or two, look for two or three motives to provide an in-depth analysis and follow the five-paragraph model.)

- Paragraphs 2–4, YOUR EVIDENCE AND EXPLANATION: Identify each motive and prove the character possesses it.

  - Begin each paragraph with a topic sentence that states a motive (topical subgroup).

  - For every motive, provide two or three significant particulars (evidence).

  - Half of your significant particulars should be quotations, each with a citation.

  - For each paragraph, follow all rules for the satisfying sandwich.

  - Note: Discuss only one motive per paragraph.

- Paragraph 5, RESTATEMENT OF YOUR THESIS: Summarize the motives that caused the murder. If you wish to recommend that one character be held more responsible than any other, you may make that recommendation, but be sure there is enough evidence.

Option #2, Character Analysis and Cause and Effect: A Magazine Profile of Caesar, the Celebrity People Love and Hate

Essay Question: Who is Caesar? American readers want to know.

Your Role: You are a reporter for *People* magazine, writing a celebrity profile after having closely observed the behavior of Caesar as well as his many fans and enemies.

continued on next page

Your Task: Pick four aspects of Caesar—two that inspire love and two that inspire hate.

Audience: Readers of *People* magazine (high school–age readers and older).

Essay Structure: Follow these guidelines to draft a good article:

- Paragraph 1, YOUR THESIS: Identify four aspects of Caesar's personality, two that inspire love and two that inspire hate.

- Paragraphs 2–5, YOUR EVIDENCE AND EXPLANATION: Prove that each of these aspects of personality exists and that each gets a love or hate reaction.

  - Begin each paragraph with a topic sentence stating the aspect (topical subgroup).

  - For every topical subgroup, provide two significant particulars (evidence).

    - One significant particular must show that Caesar possesses that aspect.

    - The other significant particular must show how people love or hate that aspect.

    - At least half of the significant particulars must be quotations, each with a citation.

  - For each paragraph, follow all rules for the satisfying sandwich.

  - Note: Discuss only one topical subgroup per paragraph.

- Paragraph 6, RESTATEMENT OF YOUR THESIS: Summarize these four important aspects of Caesar's personality.

Option #3: Definition and Evaluation: Let Me Tell You What a Hero Is

Essay Question: What is true heroism?

Your Role: You are a veteran reporter for local news media. You are covering the heroism manifested during this horrible tragedy that left so many dead. Many argue Caesar is the true hero; others, Brutus; and others, Antony. Your editor has told you to examine all three characters and judge them in an editorial. This editorial will be published under a title such as "Hero Rises above the Fray," or "True Hero Rises from Ashes," or "No Heroes to Be Found." You will defend your opinion of whether Caesar, Brutus, and/ or Antony have qualities of a true hero.

Your Task: Create a definition of heroism and evaluate Caesar, Brutus, and/or Antony by these standards. Do their actions meet the criteria you established?

Audience: Readers of local newspapers (high school–age readers and older).

Essay Structure:

- Paragraph 1, YOUR THESIS: Define true heroism by identifying at least three aspects a person must demonstrate.

- Paragraphs 2–4, YOUR EVIDENCE AND EVALUATION: Explain

continued on next page

how each of these aspects are or are not demonstrated by Caesar, Brutus, and/or Antony. Decide if one or all three can be used for your argument as heroic examples or the opposite of heroism.

- Begin each paragraph with a topic sentence that states one aspect of true heroism (topical subgroup).
- For every topical subgroup, provide at least two significant particulars (evidence).
  - At least four significant particulars must be quotations from the play, each with a citation.
  - You may also include additional examples, such as heroes from history and current events.
- For each paragraph, follow all rules for the satisfying sandwich.
- Note: Discuss only one topical subgroup per paragraph.

- Paragraph 5, YOUR RESTATEMENT OF THESIS: Summarize the aspects of true heroism that the characters did or did not demonstrate.

Prewriting

The essay question I think I will choose is: (copy entire question below):

_____

_____

_____

Three significant particulars that answer this question:

1. _____

   _____

2. _____

   _____

3. _____

   _____

What I don't know and might need help finding out:

_____

_____

_____

_____

Handout 3.5, Essay Writing Prompts for *Julius Caesar* B

Directions: Choose a prompt. Complete the Topical Subgroups & Significant Particulars Chart.

Option #1: Informational/Expository: Who Are You?

Essay Question: Who is Cassius? Who is Brutus?

Your Role: Write a psychiatrist's report after having studied the behavior of either Cassius or Brutus. These are men who murder and then commit suicide, so an analysis is in order!

Your Task: Pick one or both protagonists and identify the most important personality traits that merit psychiatric evaluation.

Essay Structure:

- Opening paragraph, YOUR THESIS: Draft a thesis statement that identifies the key personality traits (topical subgroups) of either Cassius or Brutus (or both), traits that would be of concern to a psychiatrist. (You may wish to structure this essay as a comparison of both men or focus solely on one character.)

- Body paragraphs, YOUR EVIDENCE AND EXPLANATION: Identify at least three traits of one character's personality, or if you will analyze two characters, analyze at least two traits per character.

  - Focus on one characteristic per paragraph, especially if you are comparing both men. For each characteristic, provide two significant particulars (evidence) from the play that illustrate that trait.

  - Balance your quoted evidence with citations with paraphrased examples.

  - Provide context introducing each example.

  - Comment on why these significant particulars merit psychiatric evaluation.

- Final paragraph, CONCLUSION: Summarize the traits of personality that are of concern.

Option #2, Evaluation: Whose Version of Vengeance?

Essay Question: Do some reasons for revenge have merit over others?

Your Task: Write an essay that explains why Brutus, Cassius, or Antony seeks revenge (causes and reasons), how they achieve it (means), and whether their causes or reasons, means, and consequences are justifiable. (You may focus on one man or compare two or three.)

Essay Structure:

- Paragraph 1, YOUR THESIS: Draft a thesis statement that (a) establishes standards for ends, means, and consequences for revenge, and then (b) identifies and compares two men's ends, means, and consequences.

continued on next page

- Paragraph 2, YOUR COMPARISON & EVALUATION OF CAUSES: Identify the reasons and causes for revenge. Evaluate by standards you have established. Provide a topic sentence that states the necessary topical subgroups and provide a balance of quoted and paraphrased significant particulars, context, and commentary.

- Paragraph 3, YOUR COMPARISON & EVALUATION OF MEANS: Identify the means to wreak vengeance. Evaluate by standards you have established. Provide a topic sentence that states the necessary topical subgroups and provide a balance of quoted and paraphrased significant particulars, context, and commentary.

- Paragraph 4, YOUR COMPARISON OF CONSEQUENCES: Identify the consequences of these choices. Evaluate by standards you have established. Provide a topic sentence that states the necessary topical subgroups and provide a balance of quoted and paraphrased significant particulars, context, and commentary.

- Paragraph 5, CONCLUSION: Summarize your evaluation of the causes, means, and consequences.

Option #3, Analysis: Fated, or Felled by Free Will?
Essay Question: Is fate or free will responsible for the fall of characters?
Your Task: The Elizabethans regarded stars, chance happenings, fortune, fate, and the heavens as important factors in determining the path a life would take. Yet Renaissance beliefs about the power of the individual were also taking hold, and big social and political changes made people question whether individuals were powerless. Research the Elizabethan philosophical, religious, and astrological viewpoints (recommended book: *Shakespeare Alive*), and search through the play to find references to fate and free will. When tragedy occurs, where does one place blame?
Essay Structure:

- Paragraph 1, YOUR THESIS: State whether two or more characters accept fate (as victims) or make choices of free will that lead to their tragic ends, and explain how these characters' choices show an overarching belief about fate and free will. (Note: your argument does not have to be an either/or statement but can consider how fate and free will interact).

- Body paragraphs, YOUR EVIDENCE and EXPLANATION: Demonstrate fate or free will at work. Provide topic sentences that state the necessary topical subgroups. Provide a balance of quoted and paraphrased significant particulars from both the play and your research. Offer context and commentary for all evidence.

- Final paragraph, CONCLUSION: Summarize your argument about the work of fate and/or free will in causing the play's tragedies.

Option #4, Evaluation: Judgment of a Tragedy
Essay Question: Who is to blame?

continued on next page

Your Task: Review all catastrophes and misfortunes of the play, considering how actions became tragedy. You are the historian reconstructing choices that led to three deaths: Caesar's, Brutus's, and Cassius's. Your evaluation will determine how history is written for the ages.

Essay Structure:

- Paragraph 1, YOUR THESIS: Identify those people involved in a cause-and-effect chain of decisions that leads to the tragic deaths. Name the person(s) most responsible for the tragedy, using a scale of blame that weighs whose actions are the most culpable and whose are least. (For example, you might use legal standards such as first-, second-, and third-degree murder, based on premeditation, self-defense, etc.).

- Body paragraphs: YOUR EVIDENCE & EXPLANATION: Identify the actions people choose, one after the other, that result in the tragedy, and weigh them by your standard of culpability. Provide topic sentences that state the necessary topical subgroups. Provide a balance of quoted and paraphrased significant particulars from both the play and your research. Offer context and commentary for all evidence.

- Final paragraph, CONCLUSION: Summarize the actions and their evaluation by your scale, naming the person(s) most blameworthy.

Prewriting

The essay question I think I will choose is: (copy entire question below):

_____

_____

_____

Three significant particulars that answer this question:

1. _____

   _____

2. _____

   _____

3. _____

   _____

What I don't know and might need help finding out:

_____

_____

_____

Handout: 3.5, Essay Prompts for *Julius Caesar* C

Option #1, Character Analysis and Cause and Effect: Will Power and Staying Power

Essay Question: "Wars are won by fire power, will power, and staying power," states newsman Dan Rather ("Dan Rather Reports" HD Net). Whose will and constancy are the strongest in this play? In the battle for Rome after Caesar's death, the characters of Octavius, Antony, Cassius, and Brutus show different amounts of will power and staying power. Analyze one or more of these characters' will power and staying power and how these character traits lead to the final scene of the play.

Writing Process:

1. Define will power and constancy.

2. Search *Julius Caesar* for quotations demonstrating will power and constancy.

3. Choose the characters you will analyze.

4. Gather your significant particulars and classify into topical subgroups.

5. Order your topical subgroups and map your draft.

6. Check all paragraphs for topic sentences that lead back to the previewing thesis; for substantive significant particulars that illustrate a balance of quoted and paraphrased sources from both the play and other sources; and for coherent context and commentary that makes each paragraph a satisfying sandwich.

Option #2: Analysis: "This Our Lofty Scene"

Essay Question: Is politics in Shakespeare's portrayal of ancient Rome all an act? Is the dominant M.O. (*modus operandi*) pretense and manipulation to achieve political ends?

Writing Process:

1. Identify the political goals of various characters.

2. Search the play for evidence of manipulation and deception as well as straightforward, honest behaviors employed by various characters as they achieve their political goals.

3. Choose the characters you will analyze.

4. Follow Steps 4 through 6 in Option #1.

Option #3, Character Analysis and Evaluation: May the Best Man Win

Essay Question: Who is the epitome of manhood? Antony calls Caesar "the noblest man / That ever lived in the tide of times" and Brutus, "the noblest Roman of them all." Can Antony's words be trusted? Are these men both the best of history and of Rome, and therefore do others pale in comparison?

Writing Process:

1. Research Elizabethan and ancient Roman ideals of manhood. (Shake-

continued on next page

speare is writing a fictionalized version of history, so both ideals will inform his portrayal.)

2. Search *Julius Caesar* for quotations describing standards of manhood.
3. Develop standards for manhood based on your research.
4. Choose who you will analyze—one or more characters?
5. Follow Steps 4 through 6 in Option #1.

Additional Prompts

Evaluation: What Is the Good Life?

Essay Question: Is Stoicism or Epicureanism the best life to live? Brutus is a Stoic, and Cassius, an Epicurean, until his last moments. Has either made the best choice?

Cause and Effect: Motifs

Essay Question: How do motifs suggest big ideas and produce an essential understanding, or thematic message? For example, how do nature motifs express generalizations about power?

Analysis and Evaluation: Fate or Free Will?

Essay Question: Are Cassius, Brutus, and Caesar empowered by fate or free will or disempowered by fate or free will by the end of the play?

Analysis and Evaluation: Meditations on Government

Essay Question: In his article, "The American Promise," *Newsweek* author Jon Meacham argues that "The theme that connects our triumphant and tragic past with the future now unfolding is at once the simplest and most complex of forces in human affairs: the freedom of the individual to decide his own destiny in a republic created by Madison but turned democratic by Jackson. Destiny in an Aristotelian *polis*, or city, is not only a private matter; one's values and hopes and fears are inextricably connected to the larger community. Hence liberty under law rather than liberty without constraint: that way lies madness" (48). Does *Julius Caesar* teach us that government of and by the people (a republic) is possible or impossible? Can the people in Julius Caesar's Rome handle "liberty under law" or do we see "liberty without constraint"?

Prewriting

The essay question I think I will choose is: (copy entire question below):

_____

_____

Three significant particulars that answer this question:

1. _____
2. _____
3. _____

What I don't know and might need help finding out:

_____

_____

Teaching Julius Caesar: *A Differentiated Approach* © 2010 Lyn Fairchild Hawks.

Handout 3.6, Essay Rubric			
CRITERIA	NOVICE	ON TARGET	ADVANCED
Content: The goal and purpose of writing; its main points and supporting details	The content -- makes statements but not an argument, or, neglects a thesis -- identifies some aspects of the subject but neglects others -- includes less than two significant particulars per aspect; some fit the subject -- includes very few quotations or does not appropriately paraphrase examples -- provides little context or commentary for each example -- does not keep audience in mind	The content -- offers a comprehensive thesis with some obvious statements and some insight in a mostly clear argument -- identifies multiple aspects of the subject (topical subgroups) -- includes two or more significant particulars as evidence per topical subgroup -- includes some quotations and paraphrased examples; some are appropriate and some are tangential or irrelevant -- provides some context and commentary for each example -- keeps audience in mind	The content -- argues an insightful and powerful thesis -- develops all topical subgroups thoroughly throughout the essay and shares thoughtful ideas that surprise the reader -- includes three or more well-selected quotations and paraphrased examples as significant particulars -- provides clarifying context and elaborative commentary for each example -- keeps audience in mind at all times
Structure: The organization of the essay's argument.	The structure -- lacks an overall plan or logical flow to follow -- hints at a possible thesis statement, though the thought is not complete -- has very few topic sentences or none at all -- includes particulars that repeat, overlap, or go astray, lacking significance	The structure -- follows the five-paragraph model or another logical plan -- establishes a thesis from the beginning that previews some or all of the topical subgroups (there may sometimes be a lack of precision or specificity) -- follows a clear plan established by the thesis while sometimes including unnecessary details -- provides topic sentences in some or all paragraphs	The structure -- follows the five-paragraph model or another logical structure that is seamless -- establishes a thesis from the beginning that previews all of the topical subgroups to be discussed in the essay -- makes a clear argument -- guides paragraphs with clear and compelling topic sentences
Diction: Word choice and usage	The writing -- uses a limited range of vocabulary below grade level -- overuses adverbs and adjectives instead of concrete details, or uses a limited and general range of adjectives and adverbs -- relies on repeated, general verbs rather than active verbs	The writing -- uses vocabulary near or at grade level -- uses effective adjectives and adverbs in conjunction with concrete details -- uses active verbs on occasion -- takes some risks with new diction, if not always accurate	The writing -- uses vocabulary at above grade level that is appropriate to the topic; new words are sometimes used -- balances concrete details that build effective images with timely use of adjectives and adverbs where commentary and generalization is needed -- uses power verbs
Grammar & Mechanics: **Grammar:** Rules and structural relationships **Mechanics:** Technical aspects of prose style such as punctuation	The writing suffers from several errors, including: ❑ fragments ❑ run-ons ❑ comma splices and other comma errors ❑ semicolon and colon errors ❑ misspellings	The writing generally avoids: ❑ fragments ❑ run-ons ❑ comma splices and other comma errors ❑ semicolon and colon errors ❑ misspellings	The writing avoids: ❑ fragments ❑ run-ons ❑ comma splices and other comma errors ❑ semicolon and colon errors ❑ misspellings

Teaching Julius Caesar: *A Differentiated Approach* © 2010 Lyn Fairchild Hawks.

Big Ideas in Act 3: Make Your Own Reference Guide

Identify big ideas most helpful to you and your students. Record quotations.

<table>
<tr>
<td>

The Big Idea of _____:

act 3, scene ___,

_____:

" _____

_____

_____."

</td>
<td>

The Big Idea of _____:

act 3, scene ___,

_____:

" _____

_____

_____."

</td>
</tr>
<tr>
<td>

The Big Idea of _____:

act 3, scene ___,

_____:

" _____

_____

_____."

</td>
<td>

The Big Idea of _____:

act 3, scene ___,

_____:

" _____

_____

_____."

</td>
</tr>
<tr>
<td>

The Big Idea of _____:

act 3, scene ___,

_____:

" _____

_____

_____."

</td>
<td>

The Big Idea of _____:

act 3, scene ___,

_____:

" _____

_____

_____."

</td>
</tr>
<tr>
<td>

The Big Idea of _____:

act 3, scene ___,

_____:

" _____

_____

_____."

</td>
<td>

The Big Idea of _____:

act 3, scene ___,

_____:

" _____

_____

_____."

</td>
</tr>
</table>

Acts 4 and 5

Introduction

The Philosophy behind Acts 4 and 5

Acts 4 and 5 are quick movements toward the tragic deaths of Cassius and Brutus. They are necessary scenes but lack the sweeping and climactic energy of act 3, which is fitting, considering these scenes are falling action. You can help students see what action comes before a fall when performing key moments and leading cinematic analysis. You can focus class discussion and homework on the search for essay evidence and keep essential questions as the focus of essay preparation and discussion. Finally, you will determine if the class as a whole will pursue one project in various groups or whether you will offer a range of project options.

Acts 4 and 5 are a good place to spend more class time in WCA and MR configurations while using TR groups for mini-lessons in writing instruction.

What's in Store

In this chapter you will find:

- A suggested calendar for the final two or three weeks of the unit study;
- Design tips for a lesson in plot study so students can identify steps in the falling action;
- Suggested CR passages and questions;
- Project options for your students; and
- Socratic questions for a final discussion.

Suggested Calendar

This calendar is a sample guide for pacing lessons throughout the unit.

MONDAY	TUESDAY	WEDNESDAY	THURSDAY	FRIDAY
Introduce act 4. Homework: Independent reading and essay notes	TR, MR, or WCA: Perform excerpts of act 4. Film clips. Homework: CR	TR, MR, or WCA: Perform excerpts of act 4. Film clips. Homework: Independent reading and essay notes	WCA: Introduce act 5. Homework: CR	TR, MR, or WCA: Perform excerpts of act 5. Film clips. Homework: Essay notes and outline
TR, MR, or WCA: Perform excerpts of act 5. Film clips. Homework: CR	WCA: Lesson: *What Comes Before a Fall* Perform excerpts of act 5. Film clips. Homework: Notes for Socratic seminar	TR, MR, or WCA: Socratic seminar Homework: Prepare essay notes	WCA In-class essay writing or final play assessment Homework: Project work	WCA: In-class essay writing or final play assessment Homework: Project work
WCA Project presentations	→	→	→	→

Design Tips: What Comes Before a Fall: "O, What a Fall Was There, My Countrymen!"

To help students understand the narrative structure of a Shakespeare play, cause-and-effect relationships, and outcomes of plot, present the Aristotelian/Freytag Plot Model using Handout 4.1, What Is Plot? (page 197). Or you might invite a compacting student to make a presentation on Shakespeare's five-act structure based on Aristotle's definition of tragedy. Then consider following this series of steps for plot analysis:

- Ask students to form TR pairs to perform the following tasks:
  - ELL/NOV: Use the triangle structure of the five-act tragedy to identify a key scene in each stage of plot: the exposition, rising action, crisis, falling action, and denouement. Create a triangle on a piece of paper and label each part of the triangle with the act and scene numbers (for example, 1.1, 2.4, etc.) indicating the choice for the most important scene that shows true exposition, true rising action, and so forth. Gather quotations justifying choice of scenes and write a satisfying sandwich for each act.

- OT/ADV: Decide which character choices in acts 1 and 2 lead to the crisis in act 3, and which particular character choices in acts 3 and 4 lead to the denouement of act 5. Create a cause-and-effect graphic (causing action → outcome). Gather quotations that justify evidence of a choice being a cause or an effect, and write a satisfying sandwich to summarize the effects of character choices.

- ADV: Select lines in act 5 that represent the denouement (which has the denotations of *resolution, clarification, outcome,* and *final result,* and the connotations of *untying, discovery,* and *catastrophe*). What are the outcomes and resolutions? What was untied or discovered? Choose one or more of these thematic words (resolved, clarified, discovered, etc.) to define the denouement of *Julius Caesar,* and find lines that provide evidence. Create a satisfying sandwich defending this interpretation.

▪ In WCA sharing, hear reports from the pairs in this order: ELL/NOV, OT, ADV.

- TQ, ELL/NOV: What evidence do we have that *Julius Caesar* follows the Aristotelian/Freytag model?

- TQs, OT/ADV: What caused the outcomes in the final scene? What has been resolved and discovered?

▪ This activity is a good review of the play, especially if you offer acts 4 and 5 plot quizzes.

▪ If you would like to focus the analysis on acts 4 and 5 only, consider tracking only falling action leading to the denouement, and use big ideas such as appearance, honor, and loyalty as concepts to track throughout the final scenes.

Handout 4.1, What Is Plot?

The definition of plot: A sequence of events in which each event is the cause of another that has occurred previously. German critic Gustav Freytag took the Greek philosopher Aristotle's classic structure, and he developed a diagram to help us understand how the plot of traditional narratives is organized.

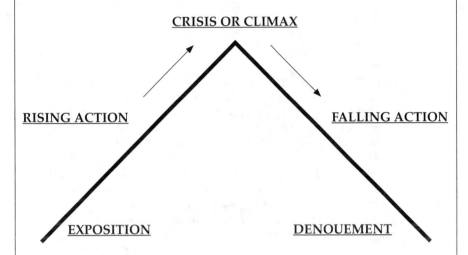

Exposition: Important background information about characters, plot, and setting, and the catalyst, an important incident that initiates the key conflict.
Rising Action: More incidents that develop the conflict.
Crisis or Climax: The point of highest intensity in the narrative where characters make crucial choices.
Falling Action: Events that are the logical outgrowth of the crisis.
Denouement: The consequences of the choices made at the crisis and during the falling action; the resolution.

- Draw a symbol of a key moment in the exposition.
- Draw a symbol of a key moment in the rising action.
- Draw a symbol of a key moment in the crisis.
- Draw a symbol of a key moment in the falling action.
- Draw a symbol of a key moment in the denouement.

Suggested Passages for CRs and Essential Questions

Note that these passages raise many questions about the nature of friendship. You may wish to convert some of these questions into relevance questions for journal prompts.

- **Antony, Octavius, scene 1 (OT):** "This is a slight, unmeritable man . . ." to ". . . Millions of mischiefs." (Big ideas: cruelty, deception, experience, hierarchy, loyalty, power, trust. Motifs: ass/donkey.) EQs: *What kind of a leader is Antony? How does he compare with Octavius? With Brutus, Cassius, and Caesar? Who is the most admirable leader of all? The least? How does realism drive Antony's choices?*

- **Brutus, Lucilius, Soldiers, Cassius, scene 2 (ELL/NOV):** "Thou hast describ'd . . ." to "Let Lucilius and Titinius guard our door." (Big ideas: appearance, deception, friendship, leadership, loyalty, temper. Motifs: heat, horses, sickness.) EQs: *What is Brutus's philosophy about friendship? What image of leadership does Brutus want to create? Are Brutus and Cassius true friends?*

- **Cassius, Brutus, scene 3 (ADV):** "That you have wrong'd me . . ." to "He'll think your mother chides, and leave you so." (Big ideas: appearance, flattery, greed, honesty, idealism, justice, realism, trust. Motifs: dagger, dogs, gods, money, metal, heat, blood, sight.) EQs: *What evolves between the two friends during the course of this scene? How do their words and actions characterize them, and how does our understanding of their complex natures deepen? Whom should we admire most after this scene, and why? Are Brutus and Cassius true friends?* (Note how this scene doubles the scene between Antony and Octavius, where Antony and Cassius both raise the question of who is the more experienced soldier. Loyalty and trust are also big ideas for these scenes that mirror relationships—one that is not a true friendship, and one that was friendship, on the verge of ending.)

My Ideas for Excerpts for CRs, from Act 4, Scene 3 and Act 5, Scenes 1–5

Find excerpts for students to analyze in CRs.

Scene _____ Lines _____ Readiness level: _____
Big ideas: _____
Motifs: _____
EQs: _____
Scene _____ Lines _____ Readiness level: _____
Big ideas: _____
Motifs: _____
EQs: _____

Scene _____ Lines _____ Readiness level: _____
Big ideas: _____
Motifs: _____
EQs: _____
Scene _____ Lines _____ Readiness level: _____
Big ideas: _____
Motifs: _____
EQs: _____
Scene _____ Lines _____ Readiness level: _____
Big ideas: _____
Motifs: _____
EQs: _____

Julius Caesar Project Options

Here are some project options for final weeks of the unit. Note that the first options is an extension of essay writing.

1. **Speaker's Corner.** *How can I persuade others to believe my point of view?* It's your chance to ascend the soapbox and persuade people to believe your side of the story. Present your essay on *Julius Caesar* as a speech to the class, rewriting it as necessary in order to include (a) rhetorical devices and (b) props.

2. **An Occasion for Persuasion.** *How can I persuade others to believe my point of view?* Write a letter or poem to someone you want to influence, on any topic the teacher approves, preferably related to a big idea of the play. Use rhetorical devices and iambic pentameter. Present your poem in a visual form (a folio or Web page), audio or video recording, or any other approved format.

3. **Streamlined Screenplay.** *How can I convert a play to film?* Film versions cut scenes from *Julius Caesar*. Now it's your turn to make the ideal film of this play. Pick the "best of" (the top ten scenes with the most important big ideas). Argue for your choices in a proposal to a Hollywood producer. Include storyboards and script excerpts with directorial notes.

4. **Motif Magic.** *How can I explain the key symbols in the play?* Dogs and lions, fire and lightning, eyes, and money: these are just some motifs recurring in *Julius Caesar*. Make a map, mobile, storyboard, or website of the play with captions that are satisfying sandwiches, explaining how the motif represents big ideas of the play.

5. **Being a Bard.** *How can I write a play in iambic pentameter?* Write a script for a one-act play in iambic pentameter, exploring a big idea. Present a scene from the play.

6. **Who Filmed It Better?** *How do I judge two different film versions of the play?* Watch the 1953 and 1970 versions of *Julius Caesar* and judge the production in the following areas: camera angles, staging, costumes/scenery, sound track, and acting. Present a written or oral comparison of scenes that work versus those that don't.

Handout 4.2, Projects for *Julius Caesar*

Directions: Choose a project that sparks your interest. Receive approval from the teacher on the project topic, and then work solo or with a partner or group. Review the rubric and then complete Handout 4.3, Project Planning Chart.

Project Rubric

Effort: There is evidence of preparation and serious time spent.   NOV   OT   ADV

Writing: All writing meets the standards of the satisfying sandwich. Writing is insightful, compelling, and creative.   NOV   OT   ADV

Visuals: Visual and artistic components are creative, neat, attractive, compelling, organized, and thematically meaningful.   NOV   OT   ADV

Performance: The presentation demonstrates poise, appropriate volume, organization, enthusiasm, and participation by all group members.   NOV   OT   ADV

Other requirements:

Comments:

Teaching Julius Caesar: *A Differentiated Approach* © 2010 Lyn Fairchild Hawks.

Handout 4.3, Project Planning Chart

Project option: _____

_____

Essential question: _____

_____

Group members (optional): _____

Ideas for project: _____

_____

_____

_____

Materials needed:

1. _____
2. _____
3. _____

Steps to complete:

1. _____
2. _____
3. _____
4. _____
5. _____
6. _____

Schedule and goals:

Day 1 _____ Day 2 _____

Day 3 _____ Day 4 _____

Handout 4.4, Shakespeare, Inc.: An Experiment in Theater and Finance, A Class Project

We at Shakespeare, Inc., a Hollywood production company, need a costume designer, stage designer, writer/director, and/or sound designer to make a new stage or film version of *Julius Caesar*. The board of directors is eager to hear your presentation, and if you are successful, you just might earn yourself $20,000—or more!

Form a working group devoted to one of these roles (i.e., a costume-making company, a stage sets company, etc.). Develop a product based on your role, and produce a high-quality array of products if you want to garner financial support.

- A costume designer must plan and draw costumes for at least three characters.

- A stage designer must develop three possible sketches for set design.

- A writer/director must plan and present acting, blocking, and staging notes for a scene of 100 to 400 lines, or she or he must write three additional monologues.

- A sound designer must create a soundtrack that uses different pieces of music and sound effects for three different scenes.

Shakespeare Inc.'s Board and Its Director

Although the teacher as board director is ultimately responsible for grading, the board does have a choice about which projects to fund. Shakespeare, Inc. has a $60,000 budget, and each project costs $20,000 to fund. Will we fund your proposal completely or partially? How will you create an excellent proposal that ensures the board will decide in your favor?

Your work as a team or as a solo artist makes a difference, too. We hire no slackers at Shakespeare, Inc. If you work as a team, all must contribute diligently and consistently. If you work alone, stay focused. Even one reminder to stay on task will result in a loss of points.

To gain the board's approbation (and to maximize your grade stock), your presentation proposal must include these three ingredients:

- *Performance*: An excerpt of your high-quality, thoughtfully constructed product, using whatever visual, sound, or kinesthetic effects best present the play. For example, a costume designer might present a fashion show or an array of sketches; a stage designer might present models or sketches; a writer/director might present a performed scene; a sound designer might present a cinematic or live acting montage, freeze-frame style, with new sound track included. Time limit: 10 minutes. The board will review this portion.

- *Written Justification*: An essay including quotations from the play and explanations, in the form of an essay (three-paragraph minimum,

continued on next page

five-paragraph maximum), to justify why these costumes/sets/lines or monologues/songs were chosen, created, and presented this way. Each company member is responsible for writing one body paragraph justifying the company's choice. Word limit: 1,000 words. The board director will review this portion.

- *Sales Pitch*: A brief speech that begins with an introduction explaining who your company is, why you are presenting, and why you deserve the grant money; a body of arguments presenting three distinct points that show how your ideas will help the play *Julius Caesar*; and a conclusion that reviews your main three points. The essay will serve as notes for your presentation. Time limit: 5 minutes. The board will review this portion.

Shakespeare, Inc., Evaluation Rubric

Project Criteria	NOVICE	ON TARGET	ADVANCED
Presentation (Sales Pitch):			
1. Introduction (who you are, why you are here, and why your company deserves the grant)			
2. Body (points effectively stated, each paragraph devoted to a clear and coherent explanation of one aspect of the presentation)			
3. Conclusion (complete summary)			
4. Polish and style (effective sales pitch)			
Product:			
1. Creativity (uniqueness) of ideas			
2. Quality (effort, thoroughness, polish)			
Essay:			
1. Organization and coherence			
2. Substantive evidence justifying each choice			
3. Rhetorical devices, diction, and voice to create a compelling argument			
Group Work or Solo Effort:			
Work ethic, dedication, focus, drive			

Comments:

Design Tips for Post-Play Poll and Final Play Assessment

In the final days of the unit, you will balance reading and plot analysis with essay preparation and Socratic discussions. You might assign a final project. The post-play poll can aid in a final Socratic discussion, and the final play assessment can be given in lieu of a final quiz or even in-class essay writing, depending on your writing goals.

Post-Play Poll

Determine where students stand now in terms of beliefs by distributing Handout 4.5, Post-Play Poll: Where Do You Stand? (page 206) for independent work, or by using the human graph activity (see act 1, page 23) to ask students to take a position in front of the class and defend it. Whether speaking or writing, students should cite specific examples (paraphrased or quoted) to defend their reasoning. How do character choices and plot outcomes further convince students of their original stance or cause them to change their positions? Note that there will be more defined answers in this exercise than in the pre-play poll, since certain arguments have more evidence than others. For example, Shakespeare does describe natural events as mirrors to the spiritual and emotional states of characters. However, other statements, such as "power corrupted Caesar" leave readers more ambivalent and require us to examine the play as a whole for evidence. Perhaps we find that power corrupted Caesar somewhat, but less so than Cassius or Antony? Is there a continuum of corruption, and some characters fall farther toward evil than others?

Final Play Assessment

The ideal performance on this assessment (page 208) is all students, no matter what their readiness level, actively engaged with annotating and translating the given section of text. Provide copies of the play that do not directly translate (for example, *No Fear* Shakespeare should not be present for this assessment). See how your students perform on this assessment as compared to their work in act 1 with Handout 1.18, Make Sense of Murellus (page 49). If you can conference with a sampling of ELL, NOV, OT, and ADV students, ask for feedback about skills and concepts they feel they have mastered, about which activities and strategies they found most helpful, and what approaches they would suggest to help them better understand and enjoy a Shakespeare play. If a majority of students in each readiness level show growth since Handout 1.18, consider your teaching of reading and writing skills successful. Make notes about how you can increase success the next time you teach this unit and in the next unit of study.

Handout 4.5, Post-Play Poll: Where Do You Stand?

Directions: Decide whether you AGREE, DISAGREE, or are UNDECIDED about the following statements as they relate to the play *Julius Caesar*.

1. Cassius and Brutus were right to assassinate Caesar in order to get a better government.

          AGREE   DISAGREE   UNDECIDED

2. The will of the Roman people always proved to be best for Rome.

          AGREE   DISAGREE   UNDECIDED

3. Caesar should have heeded the soothsayer.

          AGREE   DISAGREE   UNDECIDED

4. Power corrupted Caesar.

          AGREE   DISAGREE   UNDECIDED

5. Even though he killed Caesar, Brutus loved Caesar.

          AGREE   DISAGREE   UNDECIDED

6. Brutus's good intentions caused a hellish set of consequences.

          AGREE   DISAGREE   UNDECIDED

7. Natural events (storms, earthquakes, etc.) mirrored the spiritual and emotional state of characters.

          AGREE   DISAGREE   UNDECIDED

8. Roman leaders successfully manipulated the citizens to do their will.

          AGREE   DISAGREE   UNDECIDED

9. Money came between friends in this play.

          AGREE   DISAGREE   UNDECIDED

10. Ghosts brought warnings to the living in this play.

          AGREE   DISAGREE   UNDECIDED

11. Cassius and Brutus were right to commit suicide, rather than be killed or be slaves to Antony and Octavius.

          AGREE   DISAGREE   UNDECIDED

12. Antony and Octavius's only option for avenging Caesar was murder and war.

          AGREE   DISAGREE   UNDECIDED

continued on next page

13. The soldiers who achieved the most glory in this play were those who shed blood.

    AGREE   DISAGREE   UNDECIDED

14. Brutus was right to die for his country.

    AGREE   DISAGREE   UNDECIDED

15. Certain characters used flattery to achieve success.

    AGREE   DISAGREE   UNDECIDED

16. Honesty was a rarity in this play.

    AGREE   DISAGREE   UNDECIDED

17. Caesar was a real man.

    AGREE   DISAGREE   UNDECIDED

18. Brutus was a real man.

    AGREE   DISAGREE   UNDECIDED

19. Cassius was a real man.

    AGREE   DISAGREE   UNDECIDED

20. Antony was a real man.

    AGREE   DISAGREE   UNDECIDED

21. Portia was right to request that Brutus reveal his secrets.

    AGREE   DISAGREE   UNDECIDED

22. Brutus was right to choose Rome over Caesar, his friend.

    AGREE   DISAGREE   UNDECIDED

23. The greatest acts of deception in this play were those of self-deception.

    AGREE   DISAGREE   UNDECIDED

Journal Entry—Optional
Choose a previous statement that most interests you and explore in a journal these questions:

- Why did I answer this statement the way I did?
- Do others believe differently than I do? Why?
- How does this statement relate to my life?
- How does this statement reflect current events or the times we live in?

Teaching Julius Caesar: *A Differentiated Approach* © 2010 Lyn Fairchild Hawks.

Handout 4.6, Final Play Assessment

Name_____Period_____

This assessment is an opportunity for you to show what you have learned while reading *Julius Caesar*. Make your best effort.

Directions:

- Paraphrase the following lines into modern English. You do not need to translate word for word. You may use an approved copy of the play as well as any notes you have taken in class or at home. You may use dictionaries or glossaries available in the classroom.

- Annotate. Make notes about key words, connotations, and big ideas.

Background: Brutus has committed suicide, and Antony stands over Brutus's corpse.

Antony speaks:

TEXT	ANNOTATION /TRANSLATION
This was the noblest Roman of them all:	
All the conspirators, save only he,	
Did that they did in envy of great Caesar.	
He only, in a general honest thought	
And common good to all, made one of them.	
His life was gentle, the elements	
So mix'd in him that Nature might stand up	
And say to all the world, "This was a man!"	

Writing Prompt: Reread the passage and your annotations several times. Write a satisfying sandwich on one of the following topics:

- Option A: Analyze Brutus's or Antony's character based on this scene. Refer back to any other scenes as evidence to help explain your characterization.

- Option B: Analyze what theme this scene demonstrates, as well as any prior scenes, communicating the essential understanding you have gained about a big idea.

Teaching Julius Caesar: *A Differentiated Approach* © 2010 Lyn Fairchild Hawks.

Appendix A: Resources

Suggested Reading and Viewing

Adler, Mortimer Jerome. *The Paideia Proposal: An Educational Manifesto*. New York: Macmillan, 1982. Print.

"Ancient Rome." Google Earth. Web.

Anderson, Lorin W., and David R. Krathwohl. *A Taxonomy for Learning, Teaching, and Assessing: A Revision of Bloom's Taxonomy of Educational Objectives*. New York: Longman, 2001. Print.

Baechtel, Mark. *Shaping the Story: A Step-by-Step Guide to Writing Short Fiction*. New York: Pearson Longman, 2004. Print.

Barton, John. *Playing Shakespeare*. 1984. Athena, 2009. DVD and VHS.

Benjamin, Amy. *Differentiated Instruction: A Guide for Middle and High School Teachers*. Larchmont, New York: Eye on Education, 2002. Print.

Benthall, R. A. *The Bounding Outline: A Writer's Guide to Form and Power*. Chapel Hill: Atlantic Meridian Press, 1996. Print.

Bryson, Bill. *Shakespeare: The World as Stage*. New York: Atlas Books/Harper-Collins, 2007. Print.

Crystal, David, and Ben Crystal. *Shakespeare's Words: A Glossary and Language Companion*. London: Penguin Books, 2002. Print.

Dalton, Jane, and Lyn Fairchild. *The Compassionate Classroom: Lessons That Nurture Wisdom and Empathy*. Chicago: Zephyr Press, 2004. Print.

DeCourcy, Delia, Lyn Fairchild, and Robin Follet. *Teaching* Romeo and Juliet: *A Differentiated Approach*. Urbana, IL: NCTE, 2007. Print.

Drapeau, Patti. *Differentiated Instruction: Making It Work: A Practical Guide to Planning, Managing, and Implementing Differentiated Instruction to Meet the Needs of all Learners*. New York: Scholastic/Teaching Resources, 2004. Print.

"The Extent of the Roman Republic and Roman Empire in . . . " Web. <http://upload.wikimedia.org/wikipedia/commons/7/76/RomanEmpire_Phases.png>.

Fairchild Hawks, Lyn. *The Writer's Journey, Vol. 1*. Durham, NC: Duke University Talent Identification Program, 2007. Web. <http://www.tip.duke.edu/independent_learning/language_arts/writers_journey.html>.

Fairchild Hawks, Lyn, and Delia DeCourcy. *The Writer's Journey, Vol. 2*. Durham, NC: Duke University Talent Identification Program, 2009. Web. <http://www.tip.duke.edu/independent_learning/language_arts/writers_journey2.html>.

Hawks, Lyn. *On Demand Teaching* Romeo and Juliet: *A Differentiated Approach.* On Demand Web Seminars. Urbana, IL: NCTE. November 13, 2008.

Heacox, Diane. *Differentiating Instruction in the Regular Classroom: How to Reach and Teach All Learners, Grades 3–12.* Minneapolis, MN: Free Spirit Publishing, 2002. Print.

Julius Caesar. Dir. Stuart Burge. Commonwealth United Entertainment, 1970. Film.

Julius Caesar. Dir. Joseph L. Mankiewicz. Metro-Goldwyn-Mayer (MGM), 1953. Film.

King-Shaver, Barbara, and Alyce Hunter. *Differentiated Instruction in the English Classroom: Content, Process, Product, and Assessment.* Portsmouth, NH : Heinemann, 2003. Print.

Kise, Jane A. G. *Differentiation through Personality Types: A Framework for Instruction, Assessment, and Classroom Management.* Thousand Oaks, CA: Corwin Press, 2007. Print.

Lendering, Jona. "Tribune." *Livius.* Web. 1 Aug. 2009. <http://www.livius.org/to-ts/tribune/tribune.html>.

Lunsford, Andrea A., John J. Ruszkiewicz, and Keith Walters. *Everything's an Argument: With Readings.* Boston: Bedford/St. Martin's, 2004. Print.

Lyon, Elizabeth. *A Writer's Guide to Fiction.* New York: Perigee, 2004. Print.

North, Thomas. *Lives: Julius Caesar* by Plutarch. Perseus Digital Library. Web. <http://old.perseus.tufts.edu/JC/plutarch.north.html>.

Papp, Joseph, and Elizabeth Kirkland. *Shakespeare Alive!* New York: Bantam Books, 1988. Print.

Plutarch's *Lives.* Web. <http://classics.mit.edu/Plutarch/m_brutus.html> and <http://classics.mit.edu/Plutarch/caesar.html>.

The Purdue Online Writing Lab (OWL). Purdue University. Web. <http://owl.english.purdue.edu>.

Shakespeare, William, and John Crowther. *No Fear Shakespeare: Julius Caesar.* New York: SparkNotes, 2003. Print.

Shakespeare, William, and Roma Gill. *Julius Caesar.* Oxford School Shakespeare. Oxford: Oxford University Press, 2001. Print.

"Social Class in Ancient Rome." *Wikipedia.* Web. 1 Aug. 2009. <http://en.wikipedia.org/wiki/Social_class_in_ancient_Rome>.

Tomlinson, Carol A. *How to Differentiate Instruction in Mixed-Ability Classrooms.* 2nd ed. Alexandria, VA: Association for Supervision and Curriculum Development, 2001. Print.

Tomlinson, Carol A., and Jay McTighe. *Integrating Differentiated Instruction and Understanding by Design: Connecting Content and Kids.* Alexandria, VA: ASCD, 2006. Print.

Tomlinson, Carol A., and Cindy A. Strickland. *Differentiation in Practice: A Resource Guide for Differentiating Curriculum, Grades 9–12.* Alexandria, VA: ASCD, 2005. Print.

Wiggins, Grant P., and Jay McTighe. *Understanding by Design*. Upper Saddle River, NJ: Prentice Hall, 2005. Print.

Winebrenner, Susan, and Pamela Espeland. *Teaching Gifted Kids in the Regular Classroom: Strategies and Techniques Every Teacher Can Use to Meet the Academic Needs of the Gifted and Talented*. Minneapolis, MN: Free Spirit Publishing, 2001. Print.

Wong, Harry K., Rosemary T. Wong, and Chelonnda Seroyer. *The First Days of School: How to Be an Effective Teacher*, 4th ed. Mountain View, CA.: Harry K. Wong Publications, 2009. Print.

www.FreeRice.com

www.twitter.com

www.vocabsushi.com

The Best of the Bard on the Web

There are many excellent websites about Shakespeare. Here are some good places to begin.

Teaching Julius Caesar: *A Differentiated Approach* companion website

<http://www.lynhawks.com>
This is where you can find supplements to several lessons in this book. Log in with username (bard) and password (caesar).

Mainely Shakespeare

<http://www.mainelyshakespeare.com>
At this site you will find edited scripts and videos of student performance, useful as models for students editing the play.

No Sweat Shakespeare

<http://www.nosweatshakespeare.com> and
http://www.nosweatshakespeare.com/ebooks/modern-julius-caesar.htm
These sites provide e-book prose versions of Shakespeare's text, modern English translations, lesson ideas, quotations, blogs, and other resources.

Language: Idiomatic Idiosyncrasies. Life in Elizabethan England.

<http://elizabethan.org/compendium/8.html>
This is a language guide to help understand common usage in Shakespeare's day.

Shakespeare's Life and Times

<http://internetshakespeare.uvic.ca/Library/SLT/intro/introsubj.html>
This site offers biographical and historical information, along with links to Renaissance paintings and music.

Royal Shakespeare Company

<http://www.rsc.org.uk/explore/plays/caesar.htm>
This site offers directorial and production perspectives on *Julius Caesar*, along with other educational resources.

The Folger Shakespeare Library

<http://www.folger.edu/index.cfm>
Folger Library provides an extensive section for teachers, including lesson plan archives with lessons created and tested by classroom teachers.

Interactive Shakespeare Project

<http://www.holycross.edu/departments/theatre/projects/isp/measure/teachguide>
A collaboration between the College of Holy Cross English and theater departments, this site offers ideas for teaching meter, staging performances, and using video.

Shakespeare and the Globe: Then and Now

<http://search.eb.com/shakespeare/index2.html>
Encyclopaedia Brittanica's site includes the history of Shakespeare and other writers of his day, The Globe, the Elizabethan context, and text of all his plays. You can also find thumbnail sketches of characters, along with relevant maps, Shakespeare quizzes, a filmography, and other history related to modern productions.

About.com

<http://shakespeare.about.com>
An extensive site for the literary study of Shakespeare, including discussions and close readings of key soliloquies, an Elizabethan glossary, a quotation collection organized by theme, and plenty of history resources.

Shakespeare Resource Center

<http://www.bardweb.net/about.html>
At this site you will find Shakespearean and Elizabethan history, information on the Globe, and plenty of excellent links to other websites, especially about Shakespearean language. An analysis of Marc Antony's most famous speech is found at http://www.bardweb.net/content/readings/caesar/lines.html

Mr. William Shakespeare and the Internet

<http://shakespeare.palomar.edu>
At this site you will find history, lessons, and links.

Shakespeare Illustrated

<http://shakespeare.emory.edu/illustrated_index.cfm>
This Emory University website explores nineteenth-century paintings, criticism and productions of Shakespeare's plays, and their influences on one another. See two about *Julius Caesar* at http://shakespeare.emory.edu/illustrated_playdisplay.cfm?playid=12

Shakespeare: Subject to Change

<http://broadband.ciconline.org/shakespeare>
Cable in the Classroom offers interactive lessons on the printing process of the Bard's plays as well as variations in the performances of his work.

Shakespeare's Globe

<http://www.shakespeares-globe.org>
This is the website of the rebuilt Globe Theater at Bankside, London.

Shakespearean Tragedy by A. C. Bradley

<http://www.clicknotes.com/bradley>
Bradley's lectures on tragedy are available online.

Appendix B: Grading in a Differentiated Classroom

How you grade depends on many elements: your school's grading protocols, your district and department guidelines, state or standardized test criteria, your school's leadership, and your school's relationship with the parent community. Since you can't go this alone, consider the following approaches for grading.

1. Consult with colleagues, then department chairs, then principal(s)/head of school in the appropriate hierarchy before implementing your grading system. It is crucial that you gain support for your methods before any questions arise.

2. Identify certain assessments and assignments, such as acts 1 through 5 quizzes, as standardized assessments and assignments for the unit. Which tests represent grade-level understanding? Which assignments should all students at this grade level be able to pass (in an ideal world)?

   a. All student work on these assessments will be graded by a standard A through F rubric using grade-level standards: an "at standard" measure.

   b. Be prepared for ELL/NOV students to earn D's and F's despite progress they make during the unit and OT/ADV students to make easy A's.

   c. When you record this grade, title the assessment as standardized with an "S"—as in "S–Act 1 Quiz." It will help you see the different types of assessments at a glance and the balance of standardized to differentiated.

   d. Depending on your school's expectations, you may need to give more weight to standardized assessments than differentiated assessments.

3. Identify certain assessments and assignments as differentiated (whether TR or MR).

   a. You can use TR rubrics to grade these so that an ELL/NOV student can earn an A on an essay that meets all "A" requirements for that level (for example, an A might require the student to include two significant particulars and an accurate topic sentence. You would not fault the student for not including context, for wandering into tangential commentary, or for a lack of transitions).

    b. When you record this grade, title the assessment as differentiated with a "D"—as in "D–Final Essay."

    c. You will see every readiness level make more progress, most obvious when ELL/NOV students' grades improve while OT/ADV students' grades decline.

    d. Some might perceive this system as "unfair" because not all assessments are standardized and some will achieve mastery at their readiness level while others will be asked for the first time to stretch beyond an easy A or B. Here is where the public relations part is needed and where your department chair and administration must support you in this venture. Listen to Podcast #2 at www.readwritethink. org (see page 216) for more information on handling negative reaction to differentiated grading.

4. A tip for paper management:

    a. Decide which assignments are informal and which are formal; which ones need rubrics and which do not.

    b. Do not grade everything. To pace grading, collect one-third of the ELL, NOV, OT, and ADV work (for example, CR homework) on a regular basis so you get a sense of various readiness levels.

    c. Alternate between brief skimming of some assignments for diagnostic information and in-depth evaluation of others.

5. When talking to students about grades, use these statements to help students understand your assignments and grading.

    a. My goal is to make sure that everyone excels and everyone is challenged. My job is to ensure each of you is working at your appropriate level of challenge.

    b. No one here is identical. That means my teaching can't be one-size-fits-all. Sometimes assignments must be individualized, what we call "tiered." These assignments will challenge you at your readiness level. Some assignments must be standardized. These assignments will test you at the grade level and see where you rank when compared to the standard set for this grade.

    c. No one should experience failure or success every day. Everyone should stretch in this class, and everyone should have a chance at success.

    d. No one gets "the easy work" in this class.

    e. Some assignments you will choose, and some I will choose for you.

    f. Some assignments you will be allowed to revise. Anyone who works hard enough can improve his or her grades.

Podcasts on Tiering Assignments and Grading

Hawks, Lyn.
http://media.readwritethink.org/audio/onlinecourses/shakesdiff1.mp3

Hawks, Lyn.
http://media.readwritethink.org/audio/onlinecourses/shakesdiff2.mp3

Works Cited

Adler, Mortimer J. *How to Mark a Book*. Keene State College. Web. 10 Feb 2008. <http://academics.keene.edu/tmendham/documents/AdlerMortimerHowToMarkABook_20060802.pdf>.

Best, Michael. "Crime." *Shakespeare's Life and Times*. Internet Shakespeare Editions, University of Victoria, Victoria, BC, 2001–2005. Web. 15 Jan 2009. <http://internetshakespeare.uvic.ca/Library/SLT/history/crime.html>.

Bloom, Harold. *Shakespeare: The Invention of the Human*. New York: Riverhead Books, 1998. Print.

"Describing Shots." *Media Know All*. Ed. Karina Wilson. Media Know All: A Webguide for Media Students, 8 May 2005. Web. 30 May 2005. <http://www.mediaknowall.com/camangles.html>.

"Directing." *Cinema: How Are Hollywood Films Made?* 2005 Annenberg Media. Web. 30 May 2005. <http://www.learner.org/exhibits/cinema/directing2.html>.

Dye, Amy. "Nature and Fate in Shakespeare." William Friday Center Community Classroom Series. 18 Mar. 2008. PhD lecture.

Florey, Kitty Burns. *Sister Bernadette's Barking Dog: The Quirky History and Lost Art of Diagramming Sentences*. Orlando: Harcourt Books, 2007. Print.

Frederickson, H. George, and Jocelyn M. Johnston. *Public Management Reform and Innovation Research, Theory, and Application*. Tuscaloosa: University of Alabama Press, 1999. Print.

Gill, N. S. "The First Triumvirate and Julius Caesar: The End of the Republic—Caesar's Political Life." *About.com*. Web. <http://ancienthistory.about.com/cs/caesar1/a/caesartriumvir.htm>.

Glasser, William. *Choice Theory: A New Psychology of Personal Freedom*. New York: HarperPerennial, 1999. Print.

"Glossary of Film Terms." *The Gin Game*. PBS Hollywood Presents, 2003. Web. 30 May 2005. <http://www.pbs.org/hollywoodpresents/gingame/glossary.html>.

Hawks, Lyn. Podcast. Web. <http://media.readwritethink.org/audio/onlinecourses/shakesdiff1.mp3>.

———. Podcast. Web. <http://media.readwritethink.org/audio/onlinecourses/shakesdiff2.mp3>.

Hitchens, Christopher. "The Man Who Made Us Whole." *Newsweek* 19 Jan 2009: 57–58. Print.

Lunsford, Andrea A., John J. Ruszkiewicz, and Keith Walters. *Everything's an Argument: With Readings*. Boston: Bedford/St. Martins, 2004. Print.

Maguire, Laurie E. *Studying Shakespeare: A Guide to the Plays.* Malden, MA: Blackwell Publishing, 2004. Print.

McFee, Michael. "One-Line Poems: The Smallest Talk." *The Writer's Chronicle* 40.44 (2008): 66. Print.

"Which Modern-Day Countries Did the Roman Empire Comprise of." Image. Web. <http://www.roman-empire.net/maps/empire/extent/rome-modern-day-nations.html>.

Obama, Barack. "Inaugural Address." *ABC News.* Web. <http://abcnews.go.com/Politics/Inauguration/story?id=6689022&page=1>.

Perry, Martha, and James E. Vickers. *CliffsNotes on* Julius Caesar. New York: Wiley Publishing, 2000. Print.

Pink, Daniel H. *A Whole New Mind: Why Right-Brainers Will Rule the Future.* Riverhead Books, 2006. Print.

"Politics." *Merriam-Webster Online Dictionary.* Web. <http://www.merriam-webster.com/dictionary/politics>.

Pressley, J. M. *Shakespeare's Grammar: Rhetorical Devices.* Shakespeare Resource Center, 10 Feb. 2005. Web. 11 Oct. 2005. <http://www.bardweb.net/man.html>.

Rather, Dan. "Dan Rather Reports." *HD Net.* Web.

Seccara, Maggie. "Controlling the Uncontrollable." Elizabethan Sumptuary Statutes. Web. 15 Jan 2008. <http://elizabethan.org/sumptuary/index.html#intro>.

Shakespeare, William, and John Crowther. *Julius Caesar.* No Fear Shakespeare. New York: SparkNotes, 2003. Print.

Shakespeare, William, and Roma Gill, ed. *Julius Caesar.* Oxford: Oxford University Press, 1979. Print.

Stamberg, Susan. "Costume Designer Dips into Hollywood's Closet." *The Creative Work of Costume Designers.* National Public Radio, 22 Feb. 2007. Web. <http://www.npr.org/templates/story/story.php?storyId=7474294>.

———. "How Hollywood Makes Noise." National Public Radio, 20 Feb. 2007. Web. <http://www.npr.org/templates/story/story.php?storyId=7400850>.

Weber, Bruce. "Friends, Generals and Captains of Industry, Lend Me Your Ears." New York Times. 31 Jan. 2005. <http://www.nytimes.com/2005/01/31/theater/31shak.html?pagewanted=print&position>. Web. 24 Jan 2009.

Author

Lyn Fairchild Hawks holds a BA in English and an MA in education from Stanford University. She has taught English, creative writing, and other humanities courses for more than fifteen years in public and independent schools, and she has been an instructor of Duke University Talent Identification Program's e-Studies courses. She also has served as a gifted education resource teacher and a curriculum consultant. Currently, she is Duke TIP's Coordinator of Independent Learning, overseeing development of independent study courses for gifted youth. She has been recognized as a Distinguished Teacher with the Presidential Scholars Program, and she was a 2001 recipient of the All-USA Teacher 3rd Team Award.

Hawks is coauthor of *The Compassionate Classroom: Lessons that Nurture Wisdom and Empathy* and NCTE's *Teaching* Romeo and Juliet: *A Differentiated Approach*. Her lessons also are featured in ASCD's *Differentiation in Practice: A Resource Guide for Differentiating Curriculum, Grades 9–12*. Hawks is also author and coauthor of Duke TIP's *The Writer's Journey, Volumes 1* and *2* and *Story Writing: Spin Me a Yarn*. She is a featured writer on *FacultyShack*, an online magazine for teachers, and maintains a blog called *A Writer's Journey* that offers monthly writing prompts for English and creative writing teachers. She also has written her first novel and a short story collection, and her fiction and essays have appeared in *Relief* journal, *Stanford* magazine, and at A Room of Her Own Foundation. She lives in Chapel Hill, North Carolina, with her husband, Greg, her stepson, Henry, and her orange tabby, Sonny.

This book was typeset in Palatino and Helvetica by Barbara Frazier.
Typeface used on the cover were Copperplate Gothic and Aquinas.
The book was printed on 50-lb. Williamsburg Offset paper by Versa Press, Inc.